Mini Farming

A Complete Guide to Starting a Small Farm for Profit

(Unlock the Secrets to Growing an Abundance of Delicious Fruits in Your Own Backyard)

Larry Patrick

Published By **Kate Sanders**

Larry Patrick

All Rights Reserved

Mini Farming: A Complete Guide to Starting a Small Farm for Profit (Unlock the Secrets to Growing an Abundance of Delicious Fruits in Your Own Backyard)

ISBN 978-1-7775102-2-0

No part of this guidebook shall be reproduced in any form without permission in writing from the publisher except in the case of brief quotations embodied in critical articles or reviews.

Legal & Disclaimer

The information contained in this book is not designed to replace or take the place of any form of medicine or professional medical advice. The information in this book has been provided for educational & entertainment purposes only.

The information contained in this book has been compiled from sources deemed reliable, and it is accurate to the best of the Author's knowledge; however, the Author cannot guarantee its accuracy and validity and cannot be held liable for any errors or omissions. Changes are periodically made to this book. You must consult your doctor or get professional medical advice before using any of the suggested remedies, techniques, or information in this book.

Upon using the information contained in this book, you agree to hold harmless the Author from and against any damages, costs, and expenses, including any legal fees potentially resulting from the application of any of the information provided by this guide. This disclaimer applies to any damages or injury caused by the use and application, whether directly or indirectly, of any advice or information presented, whether for breach of contract, tort, negligence, personal injury, criminal intent, or under any other cause of action.

You agree to accept all risks of using the information presented inside this book. You need to consult a professional medical practitioner in order to ensure you are both able and healthy enough to participate in this program.

Table Of Contents

Chapter 1: Mini Farming For Beginners.... 1

Chapter 2: Understanding Soil and Composting.. 17

Chapter 3: Planting and Maintenance.... 33

Chapter 4: Maximizing Productivity 45

Chapter 5: Raising Livestock in Small Spaces... 61

Chapter 6: Small Scale Aquaponics 73

Chapter 7: Miniature Orchard................ 89

Chapter 8: Selecting the Right Location 103

Chapter 9: Choosing the Best Crops for Your Mini Farm 113

Chapter 10: Efficient Watering and Irrigation 126

Chapter 11: Raising Chickens and Small Livestock.. 139

Chapter 12: Chickens 157

Chapter 13: Goats 167

Chapter 14: Fruit Trees 181

Chapter 1: Mini Farming For Beginners

Chapter 2 of "Mini Farming for Beginners" explores the way to research your region for mini farming and create a microclimate that permits plant increase. Whether you are operating with a small outside, a balcony, or perhaps a windowsill, it's far possible to increase your private food with the right strategies and gear. This financial disaster will cowl subjects which include soil kinds, intercropping, and cover vegetation, further to how to use shade fabric and windbreaks to create a microclimate this is proper for plant increase. By the prevent of this economic catastrophe, you can have a higher understanding of a way to optimize your place for mini farming and create the best viable developing situations on your flowers.

2.1: Discussion of How to Create a Microclimate That Supports Plant Growth, Including Using Shade Cloth and Windbreaks

To create an top-rated developing surroundings on your plants, it's miles vital to take into account the microclimate of your growing area. In financial ruin 2 of "Mini Farming for Beginners," we are able to delve into the concern of a manner to create a microclimate that helps plant boom, which include using shade cloth and windbreaks.

One of the primary steps in developing a wonderful microclimate is to assess the situations for your developing place. Factors which embody temperature, humidity, slight, and wind can all have an effect at the health and boom of your plant life. Once you've got identified the environmental elements which have an impact to your growing location, you can take steps to modify them.

One way to adjust the microclimate is to use shade cloth to block out excessive daylight and decrease the temperature. This can also help to reduce moisture loss and prevent solar scorching on vegetation. Additionally, windbreaks can protect your flowers from strong winds that may harm their leaves and stems, further to lessen water loss via transpiration.

Aside from color cloth and windbreaks, there are exquisite tactics to alter the microclimate to your growing location. Using mulch, as an instance, can keep moisture and modify soil temperature.

Reflective surfaces also can be used to growth the quantity of light your plant life get preserve of, which may be especially beneficial in areas with restricted sunlight hours.

By growing a microclimate that helps plant growth, you can make sure that your plant life are wholesome and efficient. With the proper strategies and modifications, you could optimize your developing situations and gather the first-rate possible yields. In the subsequent sections of this bankruptcy, we are able to communicate in detail the superb strategies and techniques you can use to create a microclimate that helps plant boom, which incorporates using colour fabric, windbreaks, mulch, and reflective surfaces.

Intercropping is a workout of growing or greater vegetation together within the equal trouble. This approach is useful in many techniques, which include maximizing location and lowering pests. When plants are grown in close proximity, they're capable of take advantage of complementary abilties, which include certainly one of a type root depths, increase behavior, or nutrient requirements. This results in greater inexperienced use of assets and higher yields consistent with unit place.

One of the primary advantages of intercropping is that it permits you to expand more plants within the identical area. For instance, you can plant a short-growing crop like lettuce or radish among rows of slower-developing plants like tomatoes or peppers. This no longer only maximizes the usage of area but furthermore affords a natural dwelling mulch to hold soil moisture and decrease weed increase.

Intercropping can also assist to reduce pest issues for your garden. By developing awesome plant life collectively, you may create a extra various surroundings that attracts a miles wider variety of beneficial bugs, which encompass ladybugs and lacewings. These insects prey on commonplace lawn pests like aphids and spider mites, decreasing the need for chemical insecticides.

In addition to pest manipulate and location maximization, intercropping can also produce other advantages. For instance, it is able to enhance soil fertility through fixing nitrogen and decreasing soil erosion. Some crop combos also can assist to lessen infection troubles thru suppressing pathogens in the soil.

When planning your intercropping method, it is essential to consider the increase behavior and necessities of your plant life. Some flowers, consisting of corn and sunflowers, can also have a shading impact which can negatively effect neighboring flowers. Others, together with legumes, can restore nitrogen in the soil, that could gain unique plants within the rotation.

Intercropping can be a complicated approach to enforce, however it has the capability to significantly beautify the productivity and sustainability of your mini farm. With cautious planning and interest to element, you can achieve the benefits of this approach and create a greater numerous and green developing surroundings.

Another benefit of intercropping is that it could assist to lessen pest issues. When you plant an entire lot of vegetation collectively, you create a more numerous environment that is much less attractive to pests. This reduces the threat of a pest outbreak and may help to reduce the want for pesticides. In addition, a few flora have natural pest-repellent homes, and via intercropping them with other plant life, you may gain from their herbal pest manipulate talents.

To make the maximum of intercropping, it's far vital to select the proper combination of plant life. You must pick out vegetation that have complementary increase behavior, just so they do now not compete for belongings. For instance, you may plant a tall crop, collectively with corn, alongside a shorter crop, together with beans. The beans can develop up the corn stalks, which offers manual for the beans, at the same time because the beans can help to restore nitrogen within the soil, which blessings the corn.

In addition to choosing complementary plant life, it is critical to plot the format of your intercropped beds cautiously. You should set up the plants in a way that maximizes area and minimizes opposition. For example, you could use a rectangular-foot gardening layout, which entails dividing a raised bed into a grid of 1-foot squares, and planting every rectangular with a particular crop. This lets in you to increase a good sized shape of plants in a small region, whilst additionally decreasing competition between plants.

In surrender, intercropping is a treasured approach for maximizing place and lowering pest problems in your mini farm. By choosing complementary vegetation and thoroughly making plans the format of your beds, you can create a various and effective growing surroundings that advantages every you and your flora.

2.Three Overview of the Benefits and Limitations of Different Types of Soil, Including Sandy, Loamy, and Clay Soils

Soil is the foundation of any a fulfillment lawn, and unique styles of soil may have a big effect on the fitness and productiveness of your crops. There are three fundamental styles of soil: sandy, loamy, and clay soils, every with its very private set of blessings and barriers.

Sandy soil is simple to art work with and warms up rapid in the spring, making it pleasant for early season planting. It drains properly and is first-rate for flora that decide on drier situations, which include cacti, succulents, and masses of sorts of herbs. However, sandy soil has horrible water and nutrient retention, that can result in the want for frequent watering and fertilization.

Loamy soil is the proper soil kind for maximum flowers. It has a balanced combo of sand, silt, and clay, making it nicely-draining but moisture-retentive. Loamy soil is simple to paintings with and has brilliant nutrient retention, permitting flora to get entry to the vitamins they need. It is likewise much much less liable to soil erosion and compaction than sandy or clay soils. However, loamy soil can be high priced and tough to find, and it requires regular upkeep to keep its exceptional texture and nutrient balance.

Clay soil has outstanding nutrient retention and can provide a robust developing surroundings for plants. However, it can be tough to work with due to its heavy and sticky texture, and it drains poorly, main to waterlogging and root rot. To enhance clay soil, you may add natural remember quantity collectively with compost or well-rotted manure to enhance drainage and aeration.

Understanding the type of soil to your growing place is essential to reaching handiest developing situations for your flowers. With the right information and techniques, you could make the maximum of the soil type you have got got and improve its texture and nutrient content material cloth material to acquire the great viable yields.

Different varieties of soil have certainly one of a type residences that affect plant growth. Sandy soil, as an example, is nicely-draining and clean to work with, but it does not maintain water or nutrients nicely. Loamy soil, on the other hand, is a balanced blend of sand, silt, and clay and is taken into consideration the right soil for optimum flora. It is simple to paintings with, drains well, and keeps moisture and nutrients. Clay soil, alternatively, is immoderate in nutrients however is heavy and does now not drain properly, that could bring about waterlogged roots and plant pressure.

In order to decide the type of soil on your growing vicinity, you can conduct a easy soil take a look at. There are several strategies for sorting out soil, which incorporates a seen take a look at, a touch test, and a soil pH take a look at. Once you've got were given decided the form of soil you're operating with, you could make modifications to improve its texture and fertility.

For example, if you have sandy soil, you may upload herbal matter wide variety which include compost or manure to enhance its potential to keep moisture and vitamins. If you have got clay soil, you could add sand or perlite to decorate its drainage and make it less difficult to art work with.

It's critical to phrase that the shape of soil in your developing area might also additionally have an effect on the types of flowers that would thrive there. Some plants, collectively with cacti and succulents, determine upon sandy soil, on the same time as others, which include tomatoes and peppers, thrive in loamy soil. Understanding the houses of numerous soil sorts can help you choose the splendid vegetation for your developing region and optimize your growing conditions.

In addition to the soil kind, it's also vital to recall the soil's pH stage. Most vegetation pick a pH degree amongst 6.Zero and 7.Zero, but a few flowers, which include blueberries and rhododendrons, opt for extra acidic soil. If your soil's pH diploma isn't always inside the top notch variety, you can adjust it by manner of the usage of including amendments which encompass lime or sulfur.

By know-how the residences of different soil sorts and making modifications to beautify their fertility and texture, you may create vital developing conditions for your flowers and attain the tremendous feasible yields.

2.Four Explanation of How to Use Cover Crops to Improve Soil Health and Prevent Erosion

Using cowl flowers is an powerful manner to beautify soil fitness and save you erosion. Cover flowers are vegetation which is probably grown in particular to beautify soil great and offer masses of advantages for your lawn. They can assist to suppress weeds, boom soil fertility, prevent soil erosion, and upload organic remember to the soil.

To use cowl plants efficiently, you want to pick out out the right form of cover crop to your soil and developing conditions. Some cover flora are better nice to sandy soils, on the identical time as others are extra suitable for clay soils. Some cowl flowers, together with legumes, can healing nitrogen in the soil, whilst others can assist to interrupt up compacted soil.

Once you have decided for your cowl crop, you need to plant it at the right time and in the right manner. Some cover plants, in conjunction with clover, may be sown right now into the soil, even as others, together with rye, want to be planted in the fall to be effective.

To make sure that your cowl plants are a fulfillment, you want to manipulate them carefully. This may also additionally comprise cutting them lower back earlier than they go to seed, or tilling them into the soil on the proper time to maximize their advantages.

Chapter 2: Understanding Soil and Composting

Chapter 3 of our complete manual to mini farming for novices specializes in data soil and composting. This bankruptcy is an essential guide for those who need to maximize their crop yields and sell the fitness in their mini farms. Understanding the intricacies of soil and composting is important for absolutely everyone who desires to increase wholesome, nutritious flora without relying on chemical fertilizers or pesticides.

In this financial ruin, we're capable of discover the blessings of using biodynamic farming practices to enhance soil fertility and promote biodiversity. We will speak the manner to apply green manure flora to enhance soil health and prevent nutrient depletion. We will also delve into the specific varieties of composting structures and a manner to make compost tea and distinct compost-based totally completely fertilizers. By the give up of this economic catastrophe, you can have a entire knowledge of the strategies and strategies critical to create wealthy, healthful soil and sell top-rated plant increase.

Biodynamic farming is a holistic approach to agriculture that is rooted in the notion that farming want to be in concord with the herbal rhythms and cycles of the earth. This method of farming is going beyond natural practices to create a self-preserving surroundings that complements soil fertility and promotes biodiversity. Biodynamic farming focuses on the interconnectedness of all topics and seeks to create a balanced and harmonious system that permits the health and nicely-being of the soil, vegetation, animals, and those.

One of the important thing advantages of biodynamic farming is that it complements soil fertility with the aid of developing the herbal matter quantity inside the soil, enhancing soil shape, and promoting the increase of beneficial microorganisms. This is done through using compost, green manure plant life, and cowl plant life, which provide the soil with the critical nutrients it wishes to help wholesome plant increase. Biodynamic farmers additionally use natural arrangements, which includes natural teas and fermented plant extracts, to beautify soil fertility and enhance plant fitness.

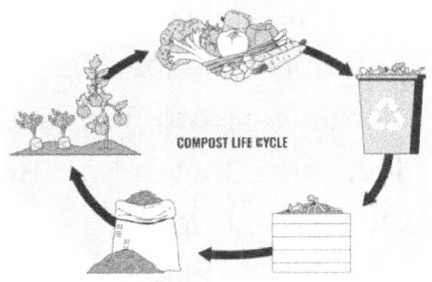

In addition to enhancing soil fertility, biodynamic farming moreover promotes biodiversity via growing a severa and interconnected atmosphere. Biodynamic farmers purpose to create a balanced device that consists of pretty a few plants, animals, and microorganisms, all of which play a function in preserving a healthful and colourful ecosystem. This approach to farming additionally emphasizes the significance of keeping heirloom kinds, which permits to maintain genetic range and save you the lack of treasured plant species.

Biodynamic farming moreover emphasizes the importance of running in harmony with the herbal rhythms and cycles of the earth. Biodynamic farmers use the degrees of the moon to decide whilst to plant and harvest plant life, and they also use biodynamic calendars to guide their farming practices. This approach to farming recognizes the interconnectedness of all topics and recognizes that the entirety inside the herbal international is installed and interdependent.

Overall, biodynamic farming is a holistic approach to agriculture that emphasizes the interconnectedness of all subjects and seeks to create a self-retaining surroundings that lets in the fitness and properly-being of the soil, plants, animals, and those. In the following sections, we are able to talk in more detail a way to examine biodynamic farming practices to your mini farm to acquire the nice viable effects.

Biodynamic farming practices can assist to create a greater harmonious and interconnected environment that helps the boom and improvement of plants. The key precept of biodynamic farming is to view the farm as an entire organism that consists of plants, animals, soil, and the encompassing surroundings. By treating the farm as a holistic entity, biodynamic farmers can create a greater sustainable and resilient device that is a whole lot less counting on outdoor inputs.

One of the principle advantages of biodynamic farming is that it enhances soil fertility. Biodynamic farmers use pretty diverse techniques to enhance the soil, which includes composting, cowl cropping, and crop rotation. These strategies help to growth the quantity of herbal depend in the soil, which in flip improves soil form, water retention, and nutrient availability. Biodynamic farmers also use arrangements made from natural materials collectively with herbs, minerals, and animal manure to enhance soil fertility and promote healthy plant increase.

Another benefit of biodynamic farming is that it promotes biodiversity. By developing a numerous and interconnected environment, biodynamic farmers can encourage the increase of a number of plant and animal species. This variety can help to create a more strong and resilient surroundings this is much less prone to pests and diseases. Biodynamic farmers moreover use strategies on the facet of accomplice planting, polyculture farming, and intercropping to create a numerous range of habitats that would assist various plant and animal life.

In addition to improving soil fertility and selling biodiversity, biodynamic farming can also assist to lessen the usage of artificial fertilizers and pesticides. By counting on natural inputs and strategies, biodynamic farmers can create a greater sustainable and self-enough tool that could be a whole lot less relying on outside inputs. This can assist to lessen the ecological impact of farming and create a extra sustainable and resilient device.

Overall, biodynamic farming practices offer plenty of benefits that can assist to create a more sustainable and interconnected farming tool. By enhancing soil fertility, promoting biodiversity, and decreasing the usage of artificial inputs, biodynamic farmers can create a greater sustainable and resilient tool this is higher capable of adapt to changing environmental conditions. In the subsequent sections, we will find out the essential component strategies and ideas of biodynamic farming in greater detail.

3.2 Discussion of a way to apply green manure plants to enhance soil fitness and prevent nutrient depletion

Green manure plant life are an powerful way to decorate soil health and prevent nutrient depletion to your mini farm. Green manure plant life are planted in maximum times to feature nutrients to the soil, increase soil herbal depend, and decorate soil shape. The plants are grown for a selected period after which modified into the soil, wherein they decompose and launch nutrients.

When deciding on green manure vegetation, it is important to select species at the manner to expand nicely in your specific region and soil conditions. Popular alternatives consist of legumes like clover and vetch, in addition to grasses like ryegrass and oats. Legumes are in particular useful as they've got the capability to recuperation nitrogen, a critical nutrient for plant increase, from the air and make it available to important plant life in the soil.

To use green manure plants, you could plant them between your primary vegetation or in the fallow season. They may be grown as cover flowers, which might be sown among primary flora, or as rotation flowers, which might be planted amongst plant life of diverse households. Cover flora can assist to guard the soil from erosion, suppress weeds, and upload vitamins to the soil. Rotation plants can help to break pest and sickness cycles, upload vitamins to the soil, and enhance soil form.

Once your green manure plant life have reached maturity, you can flip them into the soil. This approach is called inexperienced manure plowing, and it allows to launch nutrients from the decomposing plant life into the soil. Green manure vegetation can also assist to beautify soil tilth and water-defensive capability, making it simpler for flowers to get right of entry to water and nutrients.

Green manure flowers additionally may be used to save you soil erosion and decrease the want for synthetic fertilizers. They also can assist to suppress weed growth, thereby reducing the want for herbicides. Additionally, inexperienced manure flora can characteristic a cowl crop, shielding the soil from the solar and wind, and developing soil herbal rely. This, in turn, permits to improve soil form, maintain moisture, and boom the populace of beneficial microorganisms which are crucial for plant increase.

To use green manure vegetation, it's far essential to choose the proper vegetation to your weather and growing situations. Legumes like clover, peas, and beans are real choices, as they may repair nitrogen in the soil. Other suitable options consist of cereal rye, buckwheat, and oilseed radish, that can assist to lessen soil compaction and sell water infiltration. It is also critical to pick out out the right time to sow the inexperienced manure crop, as this could have an impact on the amount of biomass produced and the timing of the nitrogen launch.

Overall, the use of inexperienced manure vegetation is a sustainable and fee-

powerful manner to enhance soil fitness and fertility. By incorporating the ones plants into your crop rotation plan, you could improve the long-time period productivity of your mini farm and reduce your reliance on synthetic fertilizers and pesticides.

In precis, inexperienced manure plant life are an excellent way to beautify soil health and save you nutrient depletion in your mini farm. By choosing the right plant life and using them in a rotation or cowl crop device, you can promote soil fertility, decorate soil form, and boom your crop yields.

3.Three Overview of the blessings and obstacles of severa forms of composting systems, together with trojan horse bins and warm composting

Composting is an critical exercising in biodynamic farming. It is a natural way of recycling natural waste and growing a wealthy and nutrient-dense soil alternate. In this segment, we will offer a top stage view of the advantages and limitations of various types of composting structures, together with computer virus containers and warm composting.

Worm composting, moreover referred to as vermicomposting, is a manner of composting that uses earthworms to interrupt down herbal rely amount. It is a absolutely high-quality approach for human beings with constrained location or who need to compost indoors. Worm bins are smooth to set up and hold, and the subsequent compost is wealthy in useful microorganisms and vitamins.

Hot composting, but, is a extra traditional technique of composting that includes developing a pile of natural waste that heats up as it decomposes. The warmth allows to interrupt down the organic rely brief and successfully. Hot composting calls for extra space and strive than computer virus composting, but the ensuing compost is of immoderate first-rate and is useful for a wide style of plant life.

Both worm composting and hot composting have their advantages and obstacles. For example, laptop virus composting is good for small-scale operations and produces wonderful compost, however it is able to be time-ingesting to harvest the compost. Hot composting, rather, produces compost speedy and correctly but requires extra region and attempt to installation and preserve.

In conclusion, every malicious program composting and warm composting are effective techniques of composting which could advantage any mini farm. The desire of technique relies upon at the available vicinity, time, and resources of the farmer. With the proper composting system, mini farmers can produce nutrient-wealthy soil amendments if you want to help the growth and productiveness of their flora.

three.Four Explanation of the way to make compost tea and one-of-a-kind compost-based completely fertilizers

Compost tea and distinct compost-based totally honestly fertilizers are a high-quality way to beautify soil fitness and provide the crucial nutrients to your plants to thrive. Compost tea is made with the beneficial useful resource of soaking completed compost in water, allowing the vitamins to dissolve into the water. It can be used as a foliar spray or as a soil drench to enhance plant increase and health.

To make compost tea, you may need some devices at the side of a bucket, finished compost, and water. First, fill a bucket with water and upload a small amount of finished compost to the water. You can use a cheesecloth or burlap bag to encompass the compost. Let the compost steep in the water for numerous days, stirring every so often. The water becomes enriched with nutrients from the compost, developing a nutrient-rich tea.

Other compost-based fertilizers encompass bone meal, blood meal, and fish emulsion. Bone meal is crafted from finely ground animal bones and is a extraordinary supply of phosphorus and calcium. Blood meal is made from dried animal blood and is immoderate in nitrogen, that is vital for plant increase. Fish emulsion is made from fish waste and is rich in nitrogen, phosphorus, and potassium.

Chapter 3: Planting and Maintenance

Chapter four focuses on planting and preservation in mini farming. Once you have got prepared your mini farm and created the precise developing conditions, it's time to start planting and worrying in your plant life. This bankruptcy will offer you with precious statistics at the manner to reduce pest troubles and enhance soil fitness through crop rotation, useful insects, and accomplice planting. We may additionally speak splendid types of mulch and the manner they might gain your plants, and supply an reason of herbal pest manipulate techniques which might be stable and powerful for your mini farm. Whether you are a beginner or an professional gardener, this financial disaster will assist you broaden a wholesome and sustainable mini farm.

four.1 Introduction of the benefits of the use of crop rotation to lessen pest issues and beautify soil health

Crop rotation is a smooth but powerful approach used in farming to enhance soil fitness and decrease pest problems. The concept includes planting one-of-a-kind plants in a specific series in the equal plot of land over numerous growing seasons. The idea at the back of crop rotation is that particular plants have wonderful nutrient requirements and enchantment to fantastic pests, so alternating them lets in to lessen soil-borne sicknesses and pests that building up over the years.

There are many advantages to the usage of crop rotation on your mini farm. Firstly, it lets in to beaut fy soil health with the aid of the usage of manner of balancing the nutrient goals of plants and reducing soil depletion. Secondly, it permits to save you soil-borne pests and illnesses from setting up themselves inside the soil. This is because of the truth pests and diseases focusing on one crop are starved out while that crop isn't always planted for severa seasons. Thirdly, crop rotation can reduce the need for fertilizers and insecticides, saving you money and time in the long run.

The key to a fulfillment crop rotation is to devise in advance and pick out a series of vegetation that artwork properly collectively. It's additionally crucial to maintain in mind elements like soil kind, climate, and the type of vegetation you want to grow. With the proper planning and execution, crop rotation assist you to develop wholesome, vibrant flowers that thrive to your mini farm.

four.2 Discussion of the manner to use useful bugs and accomplice planting to govern pests with out the usage of dangerous chemicalsin severe detail

Beneficial bugs and partner planting are natural techniques that may be used to govern pests without using risky chemical materials. Beneficial insects are insects that prey on dangerous insects and might help maintain pest populations below manipulate. Some examples of beneficial bugs encompass ladybugs, lacewings, and parasitic wasps.

Companion planting involves planting special styles of plant life in near proximity to each different, in which they may be able to have a collectively useful courting. For example, planting marigolds with tomatoes can assist to repel risky nematodes, on the same time as planting basil with tomatoes can help to repel tomato hornworms.

One vital issue of the usage of useful insects and accomplice planting is to create a numerous habitat for bugs to your garden. This manner planting severa plant life, providing food and safe haven for useful bugs, and keeping off using dangerous insecticides.

Another important component is to understand which flora and insects are beneficial or unstable on your region, and to plot your planting consequently. For instance, if you stay in a place with a excessive population of Japanese beetles, you can need to plant flowers that repel them, together with garlic or chives.

By the use of beneficial insects and companion planting, you could reduce the usage of risky chemical substances in your garden and create a extra sustainable and green environment.

In addition to the use of useful insects, associate planting can also be used to govern pests with out risky chemicals. Companion planting involves planting or more crops together that advantage every high-quality in a few manner. For example, planting marigolds with veggies can repel pests and enhance soil fitness.

Another example of companion planting is planting herbs which incorporates basil and parsley with greens. These herbs not handiest repel pests however moreover attraction to useful bugs like bees and butterflies. This can help to preserve a healthy stability in your garden, wherein the useful bugs will assist to hold pest populations in test.

It's critical to phrase that not all partner planting combinations are effective, and a few may additionally furthermore sincerely have terrible outcomes. Therefore, it's miles essential to do studies and pick out partner plants which have been proven to have exceptional effects on each other. A top aid is the ebook "Carrots Love Tomatoes" by way of the usage of Louise Riotte, which gives records at the splendid plant pairings for associate planting.

Using useful insects and accomplice planting can help to maintain a healthy and balanced lawn surroundings without relying on risky chemical compounds. It additionally allows to lessen the environmental impact of insecticides and preserves the natural biodiversity of your garden.

four.Three Overview of the benefits and limitations of severa forms of mulch, collectively with straw, leaves, and grass clippings

Mulching is an essential a part of gardening, because it enables to keep moisture, suppress weeds, and regulate soil temperature. Different types of mulch can provide diverse blessings and barriers, relying at the particular dreams of your vegetation and soil.

Straw is a well-known mulch preference for plenty gardeners because it's efficiently to be had and clean to art work with. It moreover decomposes pretty rapid, including herbal keep in mind to the soil. However, straw can be difficult to anchor in area and can harbor weed seeds.

Leaves are every exclusive commonly used mulch fabric, mainly in the fall at the same time as they will be enough. They're an remarkable supply of natural be counted and can be shredded to lessen their bulk.

However, whole leaves can mat down and avoid water penetration, so it is critical to layer them gently.

Grass clippings may be a on hand mulch choice for people with a lawn. They're immoderate in nitrogen and harm down fast, but they must be used moderately to avoid overheating and smothering the soil.

Other styles of mulch materials embody timber chips, compost, or maybe rocks. Each has its unique benefits and boundaries, and it's important to remember factors like price, availability, and the unique desires of your vegetation and soil at the same time as choosing a mulch.

By choosing the right type of mulch and the use of it properly, you may create a wholesome and inexperienced garden surroundings that enables your flora' growth and minimizes weed and pest problems.

In addition to the advantages stated above, mulch also can assist to regulate soil temperature with the aid of retaining it cooler inside the summer season and hotter within the wintry weather. This is specially vital for plants that are sensitive to excessive temperatures. Mulch moreover lets in to prevent soil erosion through manner of protective the soil from heavy rain and wind.

However, there are some obstacles to the usage of mulch as nicely. If the mulch isn't finished efficaciously, it could save you water from task the soil and result in moisture pressure in plant life. Additionally, a few varieties of mulch can lure pests, such as slugs and snails, which could harm your vegetation.

To pick the right kind of mulch for your mini farm, don't forget the precise dreams of your vegetation and developing situations. For instance, in case you stay in a warmness and dry climate, you may want to use a mulch that is more proof in opposition to water loss, together with straw. On the opportunity hand, if you stay in a cooler and wetter weather, you could want to use a mulch this is more proof in opposition to pests, which encompass leaves or grass clippings.

By choosing the proper form of mulch and the use of it efficiently, you can enhance soil health and make certain the fulfillment of your mini farm crops.

four.Four Explanation of the way to use natural pest manipulate strategies, in conjunction with neem oil and garlic spray

Organic pest manage strategies are a safe and powerful manner to defend your plant life from pests with out harming the surroundings or risking your health. Neem oil and garlic spray are examples of natural pest manage techniques that may be used to control a big sort of pests.

Neem oil is derived from the neem tree and has been used for masses of years in traditional medicine and agriculture. It carries azadirachtin, that is a natural insecticide that repels and disrupts the existence cycle of many pests, together with aphids, whiteflies, and mealybugs. Neem oil is also effective in competition to fungal diseases along side powdery mildew and black spot.

Chapter 4: Maximizing Productivity

Chapter 5 specializes in maximizing productiveness in mini farming by means of manner of manner of enforcing inexperienced and sustainable practices. The monetary catastrophe highlights various techniques and strategies that may be used to obtain immoderate yields and decrease pest issues, in the end main to a more powerful and worthwhile mini farm. This economic destroy explores the use of polyculture farming, extensive gardening techniques, irrigation structures, and interplanting to maximize yield and decrease pest troubles. By adopting the ones strategies, mini farmers can produce a various kind of plant life while enhancing soil health, reducing the ecological footprint, and contributing to a more sustainable and just meals tool. This economic catastrophe offers practical insights and steerage to assist mini farmers optimize their production in a small location, the usage of sustainable and regenerative practices.

five.1 Introduction of the blessings of the usage of polyculture farming, which include lowering pest issues and improving soil fitness

Polyculture farming is an agricultural technique that includes growing more than one flowers at the same piece of land. This method is based mostly on the ideas of biodiversity, and it objectives to reduce pest problems and enhance soil fitness. Polyculture farming gives numerous benefits over monoculture farming, this is the practice of growing handiest one crop on a selected piece of land.

One of the primary advantages of polyculture farming is that it reduces pest troubles. When a couple of vegetation are grown collectively, it creates a diverse habitat this is greater proof towards pests and diseases. This is because of the reality special vegetation attraction to incredible forms of pests, and the presence of one crop can assist deter pests that could typically attack some exclusive crop. For example, a few plant life repel insects which is probably interested in others, at the same time as others can also furthermore entice natural predators of common pests.

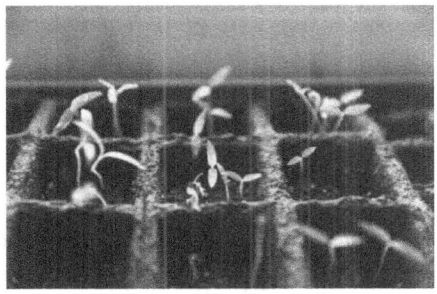

Polyculture farming moreover permits to enhance soil health. When a diverse type of vegetation is grown together, they interact with each distinct and the soil in unique procedures. This creates a extra complicated soil environment that is greater resilient to erosion, nutrient depletion, and distinctive soil issues. For instance, some flora have deep root structures that help to break up compacted soil and convey nutrients to the ground, on the same time as others have shallow roots that assist to stabilize the soil.

Another advantage of polyculture farming is that it is able to increase standard crop yield. By growing multiple vegetation together, farmers can maximize the use of vicinity and sources, foremost to a better yield consistent with unit of land. Additionally, polyculture farming can reduce the risk of crop failure because of climate activities, as particular flora might also have taken into consideration one among a kind tolerances to drought or precise severe weather situations.

In precis, polyculture farming offers severa advantages over monoculture farming, in conjunction with reduced pest problems, advanced soil health, and prolonged crop yield. This technique of farming is a extra sustainable and environmentally-friendly method to agriculture which can make a contribution to meals safety and promote biodiversity.

five.2 Discussion of the manner to apply large gardening techniques like rectangular-foot gardening to maximize area and yield

In this segment, we will communicate a way to use great gardening strategies, along with square-foot gardening, to maximize location and yield for your mini farm. Intensive gardening strategies comprise planting plants in near proximity and in a specific arrangement to boom productiveness and make the maximum efficient use of area.

Square-foot gardening is a well-known approach of extensive gardening that includes dividing a lawn bed into one-foot squares and planting a particular variety of plant life in every square, depending on the scale of the plant. This method may be specifically beneficial for small-scale gardening, because it allows you to develop a lot of vegetation in a small vicinity.

To start a square-foot lawn, first, you may want to create a lawn mattress and divide it into one-foot squares the usage of a string or timber slats. Next, you could want to fill each square with a tremendous soil combination this is rich in herbal depend wide variety and vitamins. Then, you can begin planting your flowers, following the suggestions for every plant's spacing and necessities.

In addition to square-foot gardening, one of a kind extensive gardening strategies include raised mattress gardening, vertical gardening, and container gardening. These techniques can be specially beneficial for humans with restricted location, as they will let you deve op some of flora in small areas or maybe interior.

Overall, in depth gardening techniques like rectangular-foot gardening will allow you to make the most of your mini farm vicinity and boom your yield. By planting flowers in close to proximity, you can additionally lessen the danger of weed increase, pests, and sickness, and sell healthy soil.

In addition to maximizing region and yield, extensive gardening strategies like square-foot gardening have some of other blessings. They can assist to reduce weed increase and water usage by way of using using targeted irrigation, and they can also make it less complicated to hold the lawn with the resource of the usage of lowering the want for massive weeding and soil guidance. Furthermore, widespread gardening may also need to make it possible to amplify a considerable sort of plant life in a small region, which may be in particular beneficial for those with restrained lawn area.

Square-foot gardening is a selected form of super gardening that entails dividing the garden into small, square plots, commonly one rectangular foot every. Each rectangular may be planted with a one of a kind crop or a mixture of vegetation, counting on the gardener's options. This method can assist to maximize area by using manner of planting greater vegetation in a given area, and also can make it less complex to rotate flowers from yr to three hundred and sixty five days, reducing the danger of soil-borne ailments and pests.

To get started with rectangular-foot gardening, it's far vital to devise out the garden cautiously, taking into consideration elements like light exposure, soil first rate, and water availability. Gardeners want to additionally make certain to use extremely good soil and fertilizer, and to show the garden cautiously to make sure that it's far receiving the satisfactory amount of water and nutrients.

Overall, huge gardening strategies like square-foot gardening can be a reasonably powerful manner to maximize location and yield in a small garden, even as moreover enhancing soil health and decreasing weed increase and water utilization. By cautiously planning and keeping the lawn, gardeners can revel in a large style of smooth, wholesome produce in even the smallest of regions.

five.Three Overview of the benefits and obstacles of severa forms of irrigation systems, which includes drip irrigation and overhead sprinklers

Irrigation is a important detail of any gardening or farming operation, because it enables make sure that flora get hold of the right quantity of water wanted for increase and improvement. However, there are numerous sorts of irrigation structures available, every with its very personal benefits and obstacles. In this segment, we're capable of provide a top level view of severa varieties of irrigation systems, which include drip irrigation and overhead sprinklers, their benefits, and their drawbacks.

Drip irrigation is a sort of irrigation device that offers water without delay to the bottom of a plant the use of a network of tubes and emitters. The benefits of drip irrigation include water conservation, decreased weed increase, and targeted watering that lets in vegetation growth more potent root structures. Additionally, because of the truth water is delivered right away to the plant's base, there may be lots less hazard of water evaporation or runoff, making it a greater environmentally splendid preference. However, one of the drawbacks of drip irrigation is that it is able to be extra costly and time-consuming to installation in assessment to incredible irrigation techniques.

Overhead sprinklers, instead, are a well-known irrigation tool that makes use of a network of pipes and sprinkler heads to distribute water over a large location. One of the number one benefits of overhead sprinklers is their simplicity, as they may be clean to set up and require little safety. Additionally, they're bendy and may be used for a significant shape of vegetation, alongside aspect timber and shrubs. However, overhead sprinklers can bring about water waste because of evaporation and runoff, and they also can encourage the unfold of sure plant ailments.

Other kinds of irrigation systems, which consist of flood irrigation and subsurface irrigation, also are to be had, and every has its non-public precise advantages and obstacles. Flood irrigation is a low-rate opportunity that could cover big areas of land, however it may additionally reason water waste and erosion. Subsurface irrigation is a sort of drip irrigation that provides water immediately to the plant's root sector, however it could be luxurious and hard to install.

Ultimately, the type of irrigation gadget this is excellent for a selected mini farm is based upon on various factors, together with the scale of the operation, the shape of plant life being grown, and the available water supply. By considering the benefits and limitations of different forms of irrigation structures, mini farmers may want to make an knowledgeable choice that permits them conserve water, reduce prices, and enhance crop yield.

five.Four Explanation of the way to use interplanting to maximise yield and reduce pest problems.

Interplanting is a way that involves developing a couple of plants inside the identical area, thereby maximizing yield and lowering pest troubles. This method is specially useful for small-scale farming and gardening, wherein vicinity is constrained.

One of the number one blessings of interplanting is that it permits for green use of area. By planting first-rate vegetation inside the equal vicinity, farmers can maximize the usage of available area and growth their normal yield. Additionally, interplanting can help to reduce pest problems, because the variety of flora can help to confuse and deter pests.

When the usage of interplanting, it is vital to bear in mind the compatibility of the most effective of a kind plants. Some plants can also compete for vitamins or daylight, or may moreover produce chemical compounds which might be unstable to neighboring plant life. Therefore, it's miles vital to select plants which can be properly appropriate and complementary in phrases of their developing behavior and nutritional necessities.

Another important problem to bear in mind while interplanting is the timing of planting. Crops must be planted at one in every of a type instances so that they do not all collect maturity on the equal time, taking into consideration a continuous harvest. Farmers need to furthermore do not forget the height and growth behavior of the specific flora to make certain that they do now not coloration or crowd out every other.

One famous interplanting method is referred to as companion planting, which incorporates developing plants that have a beneficial courting with each one-of-a-type. For example, a few flowers may also moreover additionally appeal to useful bugs that prey on pests, at the same time as others may additionally additionally restore nitrogen in the soil, imparting a natural supply of fertilizer for neighboring plant life.

Overall, interpolating is a treasured technique for maximizing yield and decreasing pest troubles in small-scale farming and gardening. By cautiously choosing properly matched flora and timing their planting, farmers can create a diverse and effective developing environment.

In end, Chapter five covers numerous techniques and techniques that mini farmers can use to maximize their productiveness. Polyculture farming, in depth gardening techniques like square-foot gardening and interpolating are only a few of the techniques that mini farmers can increase their yield and reduce pest problems. Additionally, the monetary spoil highlights the blessings and barriers of diverse kinds of irrigation systems and offers steering on selecting the right machine for one's mini farm. Overall, the facts on this financial ruin are critical for mini farmers who need to make the most in their available location and assets whilst accomplishing a sustainable and bountiful harvest.

Chapter 5: Raising Livestock in Small Spaces

Chapter 6 focuses on the situation of elevating cattle in small spaces, this is turning into more and more famous amongst individuals who workout mini-farming. Keeping farm animals on a small scale is an terrific way to make certain a ordinary celiver of sparkling, natural food, at the same time as furthermore minimizing environmental impact and selling animal welfare. This bankruptcy covers some of important topics, which encompass rotational grazing, herbal remedies for common cattle health issues, outstanding varieties of rabbit housing, and beekeeping. With the statistics and insights provided on this financial smash, readers is probably able to correctly enhance cattle in small areas and decorate the sustainability and productiveness in their mini farm.

6.1 Introduction of the blessings of the usage of rotational grazing to decorate soil health and reduce feed costs in element

Rotational grazing is a manner of grazing farm animals in which animals are moved amongst severa pasture areas in a deliberate and managed manner. This approach has some of advantages, together with enhancing soil fitness and decreasing feed costs.

One of the number one benefits of rotational grazing is that it could assist to enhance soil fitness. When animals are allowed to graze freely in a single place for an prolonged time frame, they may be capable of overgraze the land, main to soil erosion, nutrient depletion, and the buildup of animal waste. However, when animals are became spherical among numerous pasture regions, the land has a risk to get higher between grazing intervals, considering the accumulation of natural be counted variety, the cross back of vitamins to the soil, and the prevention of soil erosion.

In addition to enhancing soil fitness, rotational grazing also can help to lessen feed prices for farm animals farmers. By rotating animals amongst severa pasture regions, farmers can ensure that their animals have get right of access to to sparkling, splendid forage at some degree in the grazing season. This can lessen the want for high-priced supplemental feed, on the facet of hay or grain, that could help to save farmers cash ultimately.

Rotational grazing also can have a number of different benefits for livestock farmers.

For example, it is able to help to prevent overgrazing and soil compaction, that would beautify the health and productiveness of the farm animals. It also can lessen the superiority of sure health troubles in farm animals, collectively with parasitic infections and foot rot.

Overall, the benefits of rotational grazing make it an attractive opportunity for farm animals farmers who are searching for to improve the fitness and productivity of their animals while decreasing their charges. By rotating animals among numerous pasture regions, farmers can improve soil fitness, reduce feed charges, and enhance the fitness and productivity in their livestock.

Raising livestock is a worthwhile and critical part of many small-scale farms. However, preserving animals healthful can be a task, mainly without using antibiotics and special conventional capsules. One way to cope with this assignment is through using herbal treatments, together with apple cider vinegar and diatomaceous earth, that could assist to save you and cope with common livestock fitness troubles.

Apple cider vinegar is a natural remedy that has been used for masses of years to beautify fitness in human beings and animals alike. It has been discovered to have many health blessings, collectively with helping in digestion, reducing irritation, and selling the growth of useful bacteria within the gut. For farm animals, apple cider vinegar may be introduced to their consuming water to help promote normal health and save you illnesses.

Diatomaceous earth is each distinct herbal remedy that may be used to promote the health of cattle. Diatomaceous earth is a pleasing powder crafted from the fossilized stays of diatoms, a form of hard-shelled algae. It is rich in minerals and has been determined to be powerful in controlling parasites and specific pests in livestock, together with fleas, ticks, and lice. Diatomaceous earth may be added to livestock feed or used as a dusting powder to assist manage external parasites.

In addition to apple cider vinegar and diatomaceous earth, there are many outstanding herbal treatments that can be used to prevent and treat common livestock health issues. For instance, garlic may be brought to feed to assist improve the immune machine and repel parasites, and chamomile can be used to calm concerned animals.

Overall, the usage of herbal remedies may be an effective manner to promote the health of farm animals with out counting on conventional drug remedies. However, it's far important to recollect that natural remedies have to now not be used as an opportunity for veterinary care. If an animal is critically ill or injured, it's miles important to are looking for recommendation from a veterinarian for proper evaluation and treatment.

6.Three Overview of the benefits and obstacles of various forms of rabbit housing, together with cages and hutches

Rabbit housing is an critical detail of elevating rabbits in a mini farm. There are numerous kinds of rabbit housing, which includes cages and hutches, and each has its advantages and barriers.

Cages are a famous alternative for housing rabbits due to the fact they're easy to clean anc hold. They also are easy to transport round, making it feasible to shift rabbits to certainly one of a type areas of the mini farm. Cages can be made from diverse substances which consist of metal, cord mesh, or plastic. When building a cage, it's vital to make sure that the cage is solid and has sufficient area for the rabbit to move round.

Hutches are each different opportunity for housing rabbits. A hutch is a form of cage that consists of an enclosed region for the rabbit to relaxation and a separate place for the rabbit to exercising. Hutches are commonly larger than cages, and they offer rabbits extra location to transport round. They are often constructed with a sloped roof to protect the rabbit from rain and sun.

The form of rabbit housing selected depends on the gap to be had within the mini farm, the kind of rabbits to be housed, and private preference. Cages are wonderful for human beings with constrained area, at the same time as hutches are better suitable for humans with greater room.

It's vital to be conscious that the dimensions of the housing for rabbits is critical. Rabbits need enough vicinity to transport round freely, and the housing should be clean and well-ventilated. Overcrowding in rabbit housing can result in health issues and illness outbreaks.

In end, the selection of rabbit housing is predicated upon on the character's desire, available region, and the form of rabbits to be housed. It's critical to make certain that the housing is spacious, easy, and nicely-ventilated to hold the rabbits healthy and snug.

Beekeeping is a treasured addition to any small farm, because it no longer quality produces delicious honey however additionally improves pollination, which ends up in improved crop yields. In this segment, we're in a role to speak a manner to apply beekeeping to beautify pollination and enhance crop yields in element.

To begin, it is important to understand the position of bees in pollination. Bees are crucial pollinators for lots plant life, in conjunction with quit result, vegetables, and nuts. They switch pollen from the male to the lady factors of plant life, permitting the plant to breed and produce fruit. Without bees, many crops have to have a much decrease yield, making beekeeping an essential exercising for any farmer or gardener.

To use beekeeping to enhance pollination and improve crop yields, it's far vital to offer a wholesome and thriving environment for the bees. This consists of presenting a appropriate habitat, right vitamins, and protection from pesticides and other unstable chemical substances.

One of the first steps in beekeeping is to pick the proper area for the hives. The hives have to be placed in a place with large nectar and pollen resources, which encompass close to flowering plants and trees. It's moreover important to shield the hives from strong winds and excessive daylight.

Next, it is critical to provide the bees with proper vitamins. Bees require a various form of plant life for nectar and pollen, so planting a whole lot of flowering flowers and trees in the location across the hives is crucial. In addition, presenting sugar water or pollen patties can assist complement their healthy eating plan at some stage in instances of low nectar flow.

It's additionally important to shield the bees from insecticides and different volatile chemicals. This may be executed by manner of heading off the use of dangerous chemical substances on crops and surrounding regions, as well as using herbal pest control techniques which include companion planting and useful insects.

In phrases of handling the hives, regular inspections are important to make certain the health and productiveness of the bees. This includes monitoring for ailments and pests, similarly to maintaining a clean and hygienic environment.

Overall, beekeeping can be a precious addition to any small farm, providing each honey and progressed pollination for elevated crop yields. By supplying a healthy habitat, proper vitamins, and safety from harmful chemical substances, beekeeping may be a sustainable and worthwhile practice for any farmer or gardener.

Chapter 6: Small Scale Aquaponics

Chapter 7 of this e-book specializes in the idea of small-scale aquaponics, a sustainable and current manner of developing fish and veggies together in a closed tool. With the growing name for for sustainable and efficient meals manufacturing, aquaponics has emerged as a promising answer. This chapter covers the important components of small-scale aquaponics, together with its advantages, practical implementation, and boundaries. The financial ruin pursuits to educate readers on the fundamentals of this precise and present day farming tool that combines hydroponics and aquaculture.

The economic smash furthermore consists of practical recommendation on a way to set up and preserve a small-scale aquaponic system, collectively with guidelines on the way to maximise yield and control common issues which could upward push up. Overall, this bankruptcy presents an entire manual for anybody inquisitive about exploring the area of small-scale aquaponics and the manner it is able to contribute to sustainable meals manufacturing.

7.1 Introduction of the benefits of the usage of aquaponics to develop fish and veggies together in a closed device

Aquaponics is an modern-day and sustainable way of developing vegetation and fish together in a closed device. In this bankruptcy, we're able to explore the benefits of aquaponics and the way it can be used to broaden greens and fish in a jointly useful way. The financial disaster

will delve into the numerous additives of an aquaponic tool and the way they artwork together to create a self-contained surroundings that requires minimum enter from the grower.

We will talk the blessings of the use of aquaponics, which includes its capacity to provide excessive yields of fish and greens in a small place, its minimal water utilization, and its potential to get rid of the need for synthetic fertilizers and pesticides. We can also even explore the capability advantages of aquaponics in addressing food lack of confidence, selling sustainable agriculture, and reducing the carbon footprint of food manufacturing.

Aquaponics is a sustainable agricultural tool that mixes fish farming and vegetable cultivation in a closed loop. In this device, fish waste is transformed into plant vitamins thru natural bacterial methods, which are then used to feed and nourish the flowers. This results in a on the identical time beneficial relationship amongst fish and flora, wherein the fish offer a regular supply of nutrients for the vegetation and the flowers purify the water for the fish.

One of the most blessings of using aquaponics is the immoderate degree of overall performance and productivity it offers. Since the gadget is a closed loop, there can be no want to characteristic chemical fertilizers or pesticides, that could damage each the surroundings and the flora themselves. The fish offer a constant supply of nutrients for the plant life, main to rapid growth and high yields.

Another advantage is the capacity for yr-spherical production, as aquaponics may be installation indoors or outside, no matter the climate. This permits for the producing of sparkling greens and fish even in areas in which traditional farming techniques aren't viable.

Aquaponics is likewise an environmentally-first rate alternative, because it makes use of lots much less water than conventional farming strategies and produces a good buy less waste. This makes it a sustainable and charge-effective opportunity for farmers seeking to lessen their environmental impact and working expenses.

Furthermore, aquaponics can be a tremendous educational device for training the principles of sustainable agriculture and ecosystems. It gives a palms-on way to find out approximately how particular organisms interact with every other and the way to expand food in a manner that is both inexperienced and environmentally best.

Overall, aquaponics gives plenty of advantages for farmers and consumers alike, including green and efficient farming, environmental sustainability, 12 months-spherical manufacturing, and academic possibilities.

7.2 Discussion of a way to use natural pest control strategies like introducing beneficial insects to govern pests in an aquaponic device

In an aquaponic tool, pest manage is a important assignment. Introducing useful bugs can be an powerful and herbal manner to manipulate pests without using dangerous chemical substances. The reason is to create a balanced surroundings in which predatory insects will feed on pests and help hold the general fitness of the system.

Some commonplace useful insects applied in aquaponics encompass ladybugs, lacewings, and praying mantises. These insects are herbal predators of pests like aphids, whiteflies, and spider mites. They can be brought into the machine with the aid of manner of buying them from a provider or via attracting them to the device through proper habitat and meals belongings.

To entice beneficial insects, it's far crucial to offer them with a appropriate environment. This includes flowers that provide nectar, pollen, and secure haven. Flowers like marigolds, daisies, and cosmos are extremely good alternatives for attracting useful bugs. In addition, incorporating accomplice planting techniques also can help deter pests and trap useful bugs.

It is also important to keep a wholesome and easy environment within the aquaponic device. Dead plant depend and particles can enchantment to pests and make the gadget greater susceptible to illness. Regular cleaning and protection, in addition to monitoring for pest populations, can help prevent pest outbreaks and preserve the stableness of the system.

In addition to introducing beneficial bugs, physical limitations like mesh video display units and traps additionally may be used to prevent pests from getting into the system. However, it's far critical to avoid the usage of chemical pesticides in an aquaponic device, as they're capable of harm the fish and vegetation inside the closed surroundings.

Overall, the usage of herbal pest manipulate strategies like introducing beneficial insects is a sustainable and effective way to keep the fitness and productiveness of an aquaponic tool.

7.Three Overview of the advantages and barriers of various kinds of aquaponic structures, together with media-based and deep-water tradition structures

Aquaponics is a sustainable and progressive manner to expand fish and vegetables together in a closed device, with the plant life and the fish on the identical time making the maximum of every one of a kind. There are one of a kind kinds of aquaponic structures, and each has its personal benefits and obstacles. In this section, we are in a position to speak the advantages and barriers of media-based totally and deep-water culture aquaponic systems.

Media-based aquaponic systems use a developing medium, together with gravel or clay pellets, to resource the plant roots and provide a flcor for beneficial bacteria to increase. The water flows through the media, providing the flowers with vitamins and oxygen and permitting the micro organism to transform fish waste into vitamins. The fundamental benefit of media-based totally absolutely structures is that they're flexible and can be used to amplify a considerable variety of flora. Additionally, the media acts as a organic clean out, supporting to hold the water smooth and clean. However, media-primarily based systems require more safety and cleansing than other systems, because of the fact the media can emerge as clogged over time.

Deep-water culture (DWC) aquaponic systems use floating rafts to assist the plant roots and allow them to growth within the nutrient-wealthy water. In this device, the fish waste is pumped to a biofilter, in which micro organism break it down into nutrients that the flowers can use. The critical benefit of DWC structures is that they are low-protection and clean to set up. They are also very efficient at generating leafy greens, which incorporates lettuce and herbs. However, DWC systems are not as bendy as media-based totally structures and won't be appropriate for developing massive plants, which include tomatoes or cucumbers.

Regardless of the type of aquaponic machine you pick, there are various blessings to the use of aquaponics. First, aquaponics is a sustainable and environmentally friendly manner to provide meals, because it calls for an lousy lot less water and land than traditional farming strategies. Additionally, aquaponics can be executed indoors or outdoors, making it a bendy alternative for urban or rural settings. Aquaponics furthermore eliminates the want for artificial fertilizers and insecticides, decreasing the environmental effect of food production.

While aquaponics has many benefits, it is essential to have a look at some of its obstacles. Aquaponic structures can be high-priced to installation, and require a vast investment of effort and time to preserve. Additionally, now not all styles of fish and flora are appropriate for aquaponics, and it could take a few experimentation to find out the proper balance of fish and plant life on the manner to thrive in your tool. Overall, aquaponics is a promising approach of food production that offers many advantages, but it calls for careful planning and manage to obtain fulfillment.

7.Four Explanation of a way to apply aquaponics to increase a large kind of plant life, collectively with tomatoes, cucumbers, and lettuce

Aquaponics is a sustainable and inexperienced manner of growing a extremely good style of flowers that integrates hydroponics and aquaculture. In an aquaponic device, fish and plants are grown collectively in a closed-loop device in which the waste produced with the aid of fish offers the vitamins that flora want to grow. In this way, aquaponics is a honestly best instance of a closed and sustainable environment.

One of the amazing advantages of the use of aquaponics is the capacity to boom a whole lot of plant life, which incorporates tomatoes, cucumbers, lettuce, and hundreds of numerous forms of plant life. The nutrient-rich water this is created inside the aquaculture device is pumped to the hydroponic gadget, wherein the plants take in the important vitamins, casting off them from the water and purifying it. The purified water is rather to the fish tank, creating a self-preserving and environmentally top notch device.

Tomatoes are a remarkable crop to broaden in an aquaponic system because of the reality they thrive in nutrient-rich environments. The key to growing tomatoes successfully in aquaponics is to provide the flowers with the right developing conditions. This includes keeping a stable pH degree in the water, supplying proper enough mild, and making sure proper spacing among plant life.

Cucumbers are every other popular crop for aquaponics structures due to the fact they develop quick and require little maintenance. They moreover produce a excessive yield, making them a super crop for business aquaponic operations. Cucumbers require lots of water, so they may be properly-appropriate for hydroponic systems.

Lettuce is likewise a first rate crop to grow in aquaponics as it grows quick and has a excessive nutrient name for. In addition, lettuce is a low-safety crop that is straightforward to develop in hydroponic structures. With the right conditions, lettuce can be grown twelve months-round in aquaponics systems.

While aquaponics systems provide many blessings, further they've got some barriers to remember. One of the most vital challenges is keeping a solid balance of nutrients and pH ranges within the water. Additionally, aquaponic structures require cautious manipulate to make sure that the fish are healthy and the plant life are developing optimally. However, with the right understanding and planning, aquaponics may be a distinctly powerful and sustainable way of growing a number of vegetation.

In end, aquaponics offers a sustainable and modern technique to growing meals that has severa blessings over conventional farming techniques. By developing fish and vegetables in a closed tool, aquaponics receives rid of the need for chemical fertilizers and pesticides, reduces water use, and gives a ordinary supply of glowing, nutritious meals. Natural pest manipulate strategies like introducing beneficial insects can also be used to manipulate pests with out using dangerous chemical materials.

There are severa extremely good kinds of aquaponic systems, each with its personal benefits and barriers. Media-based completely definitely structures are simple and smooth to installation, at the same time as deep-water way of life systems are more complex however can beneficial aid a larger crop yield. It is critical to carefully do not forget the desires and belongings available whilst choosing an aquaponic gadget.

Chapter 7: Miniature Orchard

Chapter eight of this e-book specializes in creating a miniature orchard. Fruit bushes are an splendid addition to any mini farm, offering a supply of sparkling fruit that is each nutritious and scrumptious. In this economic wreck, we can discover the benefits of using permaculture techniques to create a self-retaining miniature orchard. We may even talk the manner to apply espalier strategies to maximize place and beautify fruit extraordinary in a small orchard, and the advantages and boundaries of numerous kinds of fruit tree pruning, at the facet of vital leader and open center pruning. Furthermore, we can explain the way to apply grafting to create a numerous variety of fruit timber in a small space. This bankruptcy will provide you with the records and device critical to create a effective and sustainable miniature orchard, permitting you to enjoy the forestall result of your exertions for future years.

8.1 Introduction of the advantages of the usage of permaculture strategies to create a self-preserving miniature orchard

Permaculture is a format device that integrates severa sustainable practices with a purpose to create self-sustaining ecosystems. Using permaculture techniques to create a miniature orchard can provide numerous advantages, every for the environment and for the individuals tending to the orchard. The advantages of permaculture techniques in miniature orchards encompass reducing the need for outside inputs, developing a diverse and resilient surroundings, and promoting soil health.

A self-retaining miniature orchard may be installed the use of permaculture thoughts which incorporates partner planting, herbal pest manage, and soil improvement techniques. Companion planting includes planting complementary species along fruit timber to sell growth and soil health, at the same time as moreover deterring pests and enhancing pollination. Natural pest manage strategies can encompass introducing beneficial bugs, further to physical boundaries which encompass netting and fencing. Soil development strategies can include using compost, mulch, and cover vegetation to improve soil shape and fertility.

By utilizing permaculture strategies, a miniature orchard can end up a thriving ecosystem that facilitates quite a few useful organisms, which incorporates birds, bugs, and soil microbes. This kind of tool can help to lessen the want for outside inputs like pesticides and artificial fertilizers, at the identical time as moreover growing a more numerous and resilient orchard. Additionally, permaculture techniques can assist to preserve water and reduce erosion, making it a extra sustainable and environmentally outstanding method to orchard control.

Overall, the use of permaculture techniques to create a self-maintaining miniature orchard can provide a lot of advantages for every the surroundings and the humans handling the orchard. By promoting natural pest manage, soil fitness, and surroundings range, a permaculture-based totally completely miniature orchard may be a effective and sustainable manner to broaden quit end result on the equal time as minimizing environmental impact.

8.2 Discussion of the way to apply espalier techniques to maximize area and enhance fruit wonderful in a small orchard

Espalier is a way of schooling fruit timber to expand in a flat, -dimensional form in opposition to a wall or trellis. This method is not best aesthetically fascinating however additionally has severa practical benefits for a small orchard. By growing fruit timber in a horizontal rather than vertical function, greater bushes may be planted in a limited location, which results in a better yield in line with square foot. Additionally, espaliered bushes are less complex to control, with better access to fruit and a decrease hazard of ailment.

To begin using espalier strategies, step one is to pick out the proper shape of fruit tree. Apples, pears, and peaches are all appropriate candidates for espalier, as they may be hardy and reply properly to pruning. Once the tree is selected, it have to be pruned to have a single stem this is then tied to a trellis or fence. Branches that increase in the incorrect path should be removed, at the identical time as those who develop horizontally or diagonally must be encouraged.

There are numerous distinct varieties of espalier styles to pick from, such as cordon, fan, and lattice. Cordon is the simplest and most commonplace shape, along with a single stem with a chain of horizontal branches. Fan espalier has a crucial stem with numerous branches that fan out in a V-form. Lattice espalier is more complicated, with a essential stem and multiple horizontal and vertical branches prepared in a grid-like sample.

Once the tree is set up, ordinary pruning is required to hold the form and maximize fruit production. Espaliered wooden want to be pruned every year all through the dormant season to eliminate any useless, diseased, or crossing branches, further to to maintain the popular form. Fertilizing and watering the tree is also important to make certain healthy increase and maximum fruit yield.

Overall, the use of espalier strategies in a small orchard can result in a higher yield in line with square foot, tons less tough manipulate, and higher fruit splendid. With careful choice, pruning, and protection, a miniature orchard can be every effective and visually attractive.

8.Three Overview of the benefits and limitations of various kinds of fruit tree pruning, which includes vast leader and open middle pruning

Fruit tree pruning is an crucial exercise in preserving a wholesome and effective orchard. There are numerous one in every of a kind strategies that orchardists can use, each with its very very own blessings and boundaries. Two of the most not unusual forms of pruning are applicable leader pruning and open middle pruning.

Central leader pruning is a way that is typically used on apple and pear wooden. It entails maintaining a unmarried upright stem or leader, this is then surrounded by means of numerous ranges of lateral branches. This type of pruning is regularly used on more youthful wood to sell sturdy predominant boom and a sturdy framework.

One of the advantages of important leader pruning is that it is able to result in a robust, solid tree form. By preserving a unmarried essential chief, the tree is advocated to increase upright and calmly spaced branches. This can assist save you branch breakage and different structural issues that could upward thrust up in extra loosely set up wooden.

Another advantage of massive chief pruning is that it could promote regular and excellent fruit production. By encouraging lightly spaced branches, the tree is capable of distribute its property greater successfully, resulting in greater uniform fruit period and remarkable.

However, there also are obstacles to number one chief pruning. One of the precept drawbacks is that it may be tough to manage the tree's period and shape. If left unpruned, critical leader timber can come to be very tall and difficult to gain. Additionally, this form of pruning may be more time-eating and tough paintings-huge than precise strategies.

Open middle pruning, however, is a method that is typically used on stone fruit wooden, together with peaches, plums, and cherries. This method includes getting rid of the essential leader and developing an open, bowl-usual cover with numerous gently spaced lateral branches.

One of the primary advantages of open middle pruning is that it could help control the tree's duration and shape extra without issues than most important chief pruning. By casting off the widespread leader, the tree is usually recommended to expand extra horizontally, that would make it less difficult to attain the fruit for harvesting.

Another benefit of open center pruning is that it could promote advanced sunlight hours and airflow at some diploma in the tree. This can assist save you sickness and pest problems, further to enhance fruit high-quality and ripening.

However, one of the obstacles of open center pruning is that it is able to result in weaker tree shape. Without a vital chief to provide form, the tree can turn out to be extra at risk of breakage and one in all a type structural troubles. Additionally, this form of pruning can now and again result in extra tough to control or uneven fruit manufacturing.

Overall, each important chief pruning and open middle pruning have their advantages and barriers, and the choice of pruning technique will rely on the particular needs and goals of the orchardist.

8.Four Explanation of a way to apply grafting to create a numerous kind of fruit wooden in a small area.

Grafting is a horticultural method used to join plant elements collectively a great manner to create a today's plant with relevant traits. This approach is usually utilized in fruit tree cultivation to create a severa form of fruit wood in a small area.

There are several benefits to the usage of grafting in fruit tree cultivation. One of the primary benefits is that it allows growers to create a tree that bears a couple of forms of fruit, that would maintain space and growth the yield of the orchard.

Grafting additionally may be used to create wooden which might be sickness-resistant or can adapt to particular soil conditions, that might enhance simple tree health and yield.

The technique of grafting includes taking a scion, that is a small department or twig from a preferred kind of fruit tree, and attaching it to a rootstock, this is the lower part of the graft union. The scion is chosen for its proper developments, at the side of fruit great or ailment resistance. The rootstock is selected for its appropriate developments, which includes resistance to soil-borne pests or tolerance to environmental stresses.

There are numerous one-of-a-kind styles of grafting strategies that can be implemented in fruit tree cultivation. Some of the most commonplace techniques consist of whip grafting, cleft grafting, and bark grafting. Each technique requires top notch machine and abilities, but all involve reducing the scion and rootstock at precise angles and then binding the 2 quantities together.

Once the grafting is whole, the plant will want time to heal and broaden. This can take numerous months, inside the course of which era the grower must ensure that the plant is stored in a appropriate environment, with top enough slight, water, and vitamins. Once the graft union has absolutely formed and the plant is set up, it may be transplanted to its eternal region inside the orchard.

While there are numerous blessings to the use of grafting in fruit tree cultivation, there are also some limitations to keep in mind. Grafting can be a difficult and time-ingesting approach, requiring specialised competencies and equipment. Additionally, there can be a danger of failure if the graft union does no longer shape nicely, which could bring about the lack of the scion or the entire tree.

Overall, grafting is a valuable method in fruit tree cultivation that could assist growers to create a numerous form of wooden with proper inclinations. By using grafting, growers can maximize place and increase the yield in their orchard, whilst furthermore improving tree health and sickness resistance. With cautious choice of scion and rootstock and proper care in the end of the healing manner, grafting can be a precious addition to any miniature orchard.

Chapter 8: Selecting the Right Location

Selecting the right region for mini farming is vital to the fulfillment of your undertaking. Here's a step-thru-step manual that will help you make the exquisite desire:

1. Sunlight: Choose a location with enough daytime exposure, preferably receiving at least 6-8 hours of direct daytime every day. Sunlight is important for plant increase and productiveness.

2. Soil Quality: Assess the soil super in the capability area. Conduct a soil check to decide pH tiers, nutrient content material, and drainage. Well-draining, fertile soil is good for a success mini farming.

3. Proximity to Water: Ensure easy get right of entry to to a water deliver for irrigation. Watering is a key trouble of farming, so having a handy water supply will make the approach greater green.

4. Wind Exposure: Consider the wind styles in the area. Excessive wind can harm flowers and bring about moisture loss, so having a few herbal windbreaks or barriers may be useful.

five. Space Availability: Evaluate the to be had area on your mini farm. While mini farming specializes in place efficiency, having sufficient room for your chosen plants and gardening structures is important.

6. Microclimates: Observe microclimates inside the ability region. Some spots might be warmer or cooler than others, that would have an effect at the sorts of flora you can increase and the planting time desk.

7. Shade and Sun: Balance the need for daytime with a bit of coloration. Certain plants benefit from partial shade, so

having a mixture of sun-exposed and shaded areas can be first rate.

8. Accessibility: Ensure the vicinity is without problems to be had so that you can usually commonly generally tend to the farm often. Being able to attain your plant life and hold the farm clearly will contribute to its success.

nine. Local Regulations: Check neighborhood zoning and land use policies. Some areas might have policies on farming sports activities, in particular in city or suburban environments.

10. Wildlife and Pests: Consider the presence of natural world and capability pest troubles. If the area has a statistics of specific pests, you could need to take preventive measures.

eleven. Future Expansion: Think about the functionality for destiny growth. While you may start small, having the choice to increase your mini farm as your capabilities and pastimes increase may be valuable.

Remember that the proper place can range depending at the unique plant life and animals you intend to encompass into your mini farm. Careful planning and remark will assist you choose a place that maximizes productivity and guarantees a a success mini farming enjoy.

ESSENTIAL TOOLS AND EQUIPMENT

In mini farming, having the right tools and device can notably decorate your overall performance and productivity. Here's a list of critical equipment and device you will in all likelihood need:

1. Hand Tools:

Shovels

Rakes

Hoes

Garden forks

Hand trowels

Pruners

Weeding equipment

2. Watering Tools:

Garden hose or watering can

Sprinklers or drip irrigation device

Water timers for automatic watering

3. Planting and Seeding Tools:

Seed trays and seedling pots

Seed spreaders

Plant markers or labels

Dibbers or transplanters

four. Soil Care Tools:

Wheelbarrow or garden cart for moving soil and compost

Compost bin or pile

Soil trying out kit

5. Protection and Pest Control:

Garden netting or row covers

Insect traps or sticky tape

Organic pest manipulate answers

6. Pruning and Trellising Tools:

Trellis systems or stakes

Pruning shears or scissors

7. Harvesting Tools:

Harvest baskets or containers

Pruning shears or scissors for harvesting

eight. Storage and Organization:

Tool shed or garage place

Tool rack or organizer

9. Personal Protection:

Gardening gloves

Sun hat and sunscreen

Proper footwear

10. Optional Tools for Small Livestock:

Chicken coop or small animal safe haven

Feeders and waterers

Egg collection tools (for chickens)

eleven. Optional Tools for Composting:

Compost packing containers or tumblers

Pitchfork for turning compost

12. Optional Tools for Vertical Gardening:

Vertical lawn systems

Planters or placing baskets

Remember that the suitable equipment you want can range based absolutely mostly on the scale of your mini farm, the styles of vegetation you're developing, and any extra functions you incorporate. It's an amazing concept first of all the basics and little by little add system as wanted. Investing in excellent tools could make your mini farming experience greater amusing and a success.

SOIL PREPARATION AND FERTILIZATION

Soil coaching and fertilization are crucial steps in mini farming to create a fertile and nourishing surroundings on your vegetation. Here's what they contain:

Soil Preparation:

1. Clearing and Cleaning: Begin with the beneficial aid of getting rid of any weeds, rocks, or particles from the planting location. This guarantees a smooth space on your vegetation to develop.

2. Tilling or Digging: Use a shovel, hoe, or tiller to break up the soil. This improves aeration and drainage at the identical time as making it less difficult for plant roots to penetrate the soil.

three. Amending Soil: Based on your soil check consequences, add crucial amendments. These may additionally additionally embody compost, elderly manure, peat moss, and unique herbal depend to decorate soil form and fertility.

4. Creating Raised Beds: Consider constructing raised beds, which provide better drainage and save you soil compaction. Fill the beds with a mixture of compost, soil, and amendments.

five. Leveling and Smoothing: Ensure the soil floor is degree and smooth. This makes planting and irrigation greater ordinary.

Fertilization:

1. Understand Nutrient Needs: Different flora have diverse nutrient requirements. Understand the nutrient wishes of the vegetation you are developing.

2. Organic Fertilizers: Focus on the use of herbal fertilizers, at the side of compost, properly-rotted manure, and natural plant-based fertilizers. These decorate the soil and beautify its lengthy-term fitness.

3. Compost Application: Spread a layer of compost over the planting area earlier than planting. Compost gives a slow release of nutrients and complements soil shape.

4. Top-Dressing: During the developing season, preserve in thoughts top-dressing with compost or a balanced natural fertilizer to replenish vitamins.

Chapter 9: Choosing the Best Crops for Your Mini Farm

Selecting the right plants on your mini farm consists of thinking about factors like your weather, to be had area, and personal alternatives. Here's a step-through the usage of-step manual to help you pick out the incredible flowers:

1. Know Your Climate: Research your neighborhood climate area, which include frost dates, not unusual temperatures, and rainfall styles. Choose flora that thrive on your climate to ensure a success boom.

2. Assess Available Space: Determine the size and layout of your mini farm. Consider whether or no longer or not you have were given were given raised beds, packing containers, vertical region, or open floor. Some flowers require greater location than others.

3. Consider Growing Season: Different flowers have various developing seasons. Choose flowers that align collectively collectively along with your place's growing season length. Short-season plant life is probably appropriate for cooler climates, on the identical time as longer-season flowers are better for hotter regions.

four. Evaluate Sunlight: Observe the sunlight hours styles on your growing location. Some plant life need full sun, on the same time as others can tolerate partial color. Plan your plants for that reason primarily based at the to be had sunlight.

5. Soil Type: Understand your soil's composition and pH. Some flora pick out acidic soil, at the equal time as others thrive in alkaline soil. Choose vegetation that during form your soil's tendencies or amend the soil therefore.

6. Personal Preferences: Consider your family's dietary options and eating behavior. Grow plant life you revel in ingesting and which might be precious to you.

7. Succession Planting: Opt for flora that can be planted successively, permitting you to have non-forestall harvests during the growing season.

eight. Crop Rotation: Plan for crop rotation to save you soil-borne illnesses and hold soil fertility. Choose plants from unique plant households for each planting season.

nine. Companion Planting: Research associate flora that develop properly collectively. Some flora can enhance every different's boom or repel pests at the equal time as planted in proximity.

10. Yield and Productivity: Some vegetation offer better yields in constrained place. Consider the

productivity of the crops to make the maximum of your mini farm's region.

eleven. Disease and Pest Resistance: Choose flowers which is probably less vulnerable to common pests and diseases to your area. This reduces the want for chemical interventions.

12. Local Market Demand: If you are making plans to sell your produce, research neighborhood marketplace demand for sure flowers. Popular and area of interest flora can every be worthwhile.

thirteen. Experimentation: Don't be afraid to test with pretty a few plants. This permit you to study what grows superb in your mini farm's environment.

14. Adapt Over Time: As you gain revel in, be open to adapting your crop choices primarily based completely on your observations and studying. Your mini

farming abilities will evolve, and your crop picks can too.

Ultimately, the incredible vegetation to your mini farm might be a aggregate of what fits your developing conditions, possibilities, and goals. Start with a mixture of flowers and step by step refine your alternatives as you study more approximately what works quality to your particular environment.

PLANTING TECHNIQUES AND SEEDLINGS

Planting techniques and seedling care are vital for a hit mini farming. Here's a manual that will help you get started out:

Planting Techniques:

1. Direct Seeding: Some flora can be sown at once into the soil in which they will boom. Follow the recommended intensity and spacing for every crop.

2. Transplanting: Start seeds indoors or purchase seedlings from a nursery. Transplant seedlings into your mini farm after they have advanced a robust root device.

3. Succession Planting: Plant in successive batches to boom your harvest. For example, sow a cutting-edge batch of seeds every few weeks to make sure a non-forestall supply.

four. Companion Planting: Pair nicely matched flora together to enhance increase and deter pests. Research which flora artwork nicely together.

5. Interplanting: Maximize area by using manner of planting smaller plants amongst huge ones. For example, plant lettuce among tomato flora.

Seedling Care:

1. Starting Seeds: If starting seeds interior, use seed trays or small boxes with well-draining soil. Keep them beneath develop lights or near a sunny window.

2. Hardening Off: Gradually acclimate indoor seedlings to out of doors conditions with the resource of revealing them to daylight and wind for developing durations over severa days.

3. Transplanting Seedlings: When transplanting seedlings, take care of them lightly to keep away from destructive roots. Dig a hollow slightly large than the muse ball, plant on the same intensity because the field, and water properly.

4. Watering: Keep the soil constantly wet however not waterlogged after transplanting. Water lightly to save you stressful the roots.

five. Mulching: Apply mulch spherical seedlings to preserve moisture, regulate soil temperature, and suppress weeds.

6. Support Structures: For vining or tall plant life, installation trellises, stakes, or cages to offer resource and save you crowding.

7. Thinning: If you have planted seeds right away, thin out overcrowded seedlings to permit right spacing and avoid opposition for nutrients.

8. Fertilization: Apply diluted liquid fertilizer some weeks after transplanting to offer seedlings a in addition nutrient decorate.

nine. Protection: Shield younger seedlings from immoderate climate situations, pests, and animals the use of row covers, netting, or extraordinary protective measures.

10. Monitoring: Regularly examine your seedlings for signs and symptoms of pests, illnesses, or nutrient deficiencies. Address problems right away to make certain healthful boom.

Remember, each plant has its non-public unique planting intensity, spacing, and care requirements. Always speak to seed packets or dependable gardening sources for correct facts. With exercise, you may end up greater professional at planting and nurturing seedlings for a a fulfillment mini farming enjoy.

ORGANIC PEST AND WEED CONTROL

Organic pest and weed manage techniques are essential in mini farming to preserve the fitness of your vegetation with out resorting to chemical interventions. Here are powerful strategies for every:

Organic Pest Control

1. Companion Planting: Plant pest-repellent flowers near inclined plant life. For example, marigolds can deter aphids, and garlic can repel numerous pests.

2. Beneficial Insects: Introduce beneficial insects like ladybugs, lacewings, and parasitic wasps that prey on risky pests.

three. Hand Picking: Physically remove pests from plants. Check flowers regularly to seize and cast off pests in advance than they multiply.

4. Row Covers: Use mild-weight fabric covers to create a physical barrier that stops pests from carrying out your flowers.

5. Neem Oil: Neem oil is an powerful herbal insecticide that disrupts pests' increase and behavior.

6. Insecticidal Soap: Mild cleansing cleaning soap answers may be sprayed on

flora to suffocate easy-bodied insects like aphids and mites.

7. Diatomaceous Earth: Sprinkle diatomaceous earth spherical plants to deter crawling bugs. It's abrasive to their exoskeletons.

eight. Garlic and Chili Sprays: Create home made sprays the usage of garlic, chili peppers, and water. These can deter pests with their strong odors.

9. Floating Row Covers: These moderate-weight covers protect plants from pests on the identical time as allowing sunlight and water to attain them.

Organic Weed Control

1. Mulching: Apply herbal mulch (straw, timber chips) round plant life to suppress weeds via blockading daylight hours and reducing their increase.

2. Hand Pulling: Regularly check out and hand-pull weeds while they are small. Be nice to cast off the whole root device.

three. Hoeing: Use a hoe to cut weeds surely below the soil surface, disrupting their boom. This works properly for annual weeds.

4. Cover Crops: Plant cowl flowers like clover or vetch in between developing seasons to smother weeds and decorate soil health.

5. Vinegar Spray: A answer of vinegar, water, and a bit of dish cleansing soap can be sprayed on weeds to kill them.

6. Boiling Water: Pour boiling water without delay onto weeds to kill them. Be careful not to splash nearby plants.

7. Corn Gluten Meal: This natural byproduct of corn processing may be used

as a pre-emergent herbicide to save you weed seed germination.

8. Flame Weeding: Use a propane torch to bypass flames over weeds, successfully scorching them. This approach is first rate for driveways and walkways.

Remember that a aggregate of strategies frequently works excellent. Implementing proper sanitation practices, selling healthy soil, and retaining a various and balanced surroundings for your mini farm will make contributions to herbal pest and weed manipulate.

Chapter 10: Efficient Watering and Irrigation

Efficient watering and irrigation are essential elements of mini farming to make sure your plants gain the right quantity of water without waste. Here's a proof of how to attain green watering:

1. Watering Techniques

Drip Irrigation: Drip structures deliver water directly to the bottom of flowers, minimizing water loss thru evaporation and ensuring roots accumulate actual enough moisture.

Soaker Hoses: These hoses release water alongside their length, soaking the soil steadily. They're powerful for rows of flora or raised beds.

Hand Watering: Use a watering can or hose with a nozzle to aim the inspiration area of each plant. Avoid watering the foliage, as this may promote ailment.

2. Timing

Morning Watering: Water inside the early morning on the equal time as temperatures are cooler and winds are calmer. This minimizes evaporation and offers flora time to take in moisture in advance than the warmth of the day.

Avoid Evening Watering: Watering inside the night can result in prolonged leaf wetness, that allows you to growth the danger of fungal ailments.

3. Monitoring and Adjusting

Soil Moisture Testing: Regularly test soil moisture degrees via sticking your finger into the soil. Water even as the top inch or so feels dry to touch.

Use a Moisture Meter: Consider using a moisture meter to efficiently diploma soil moisture levels.

Observation: Pay hobby to the arrival of your flora. Wilting, yellowing leaves, or slowed increase can propose each overwatering or underwatering.

4. Water Conservation

Mulching: Apply mulch round plants to preserve soil moisture, reduce evaporation, and suppress weed growth.

Rain Barrels: Collect rainwater in barrels to apply for irrigation, decreasing reliance on tap water.

Group Plants: Plant vegetation with similar water dreams close to together to make irrigation extra targeted and efficient.

five. Avoid Overwatering

Proper Drainage: Ensure your planting region has right drainage to save you waterlogged soil.

Deep Watering: Water deeply and masses much less regularly to encourage plant roots to expand deeper into the soil.

Succulent Growth: Overwatering can cause susceptible, succulent growth it's far extra at risk of pests and illnesses.

Efficient watering ensures wholesome plant boom whilst defensive water resources. Adjust your watering practices based on climate situations, plant kinds, and the precise needs of your mini farm. Regular observation and a conscious technique to irrigation will contribute on your success as a mini farmer.

MAXIMIZING SPACE WITH VERTICAL GARDENING

Maximizing vicinity with vertical gardening is a clever technique in mini farming that allows you to grow more vegetation in a constrained vicinity with the useful resource of manner of the usage of vertical surfaces. Here's how it works:

1. Types of Vertical Gardening

Trellises and Arbors: Install trellises or arbors to assist mountaineering flowers like tomatoes, cucumbers, beans, and peas. These plant life develop vertically, saving horizontal region.

Vertical Planters: Use wall-installed planters, pocket planters, or placing baskets to broaden herbs, small vegetables, or flowers vertically on fences, partitions, or balconies.

Vertical Structures: Create custom structures like vertical pallet gardens, stacked crates, or shelving devices to cope with flora at numerous heights.

2. Benefits of Vertical Gardening

Space Efficiency: Vertical gardening maximizes using available area, making it tremendous for small regions like balconies, patios, or town gardens.

Increased Yield: By developing vertically, you could growth the quantity of flowers within the same footprint, major to higher yields.

Sunlight Optimization: Vertical gardening permits plant life to benefit extra sunlight hours as they boom upward, even in regions with limited direct sun exposure.

Reduced Pest Issues: Elevated flora are less at risk of soil-borne pests and ailments, enhancing the general fitness of your vegetation.

Aesthetics: Vertical gardens upload a visually attractive and colorful element to your mini farm, turning partitions and fences into dwelling inexperienced regions.

three. Vertical Garden Plant Selection

Climbing Plants: Choose flowers that in reality climb or may be professional vertically, together with beans, peas, cucumbers, squash, and positive forms of tomatoes.

Compact Varieties: Opt for compact styles of greens and herbs that would thrive in smaller regions.

four. Tips for Successful Vertical Gardening

Sturdy Support: Ensure your vertical structures are well-constructed and able to supporting the burden of developing vegetation.

Proper Spacing: Pay interest to plant spacing to save you overcrowding, which could save you boom and airflow.

Regular Pruning: Prune extra growth and do away with vain or diseased foliage to keep plant fitness and save you overcrowding.

Secure Vines: As mountain climbing plant life develop, gently sturdy them to trellises or enables to guide their upward growth.

Watering Considerations: Monitor water goals carefully, as vertical gardens would likely dry out more fast. Drip irrigation or self-watering structures may be useful.

Vertical gardening not handiest optimizes region but moreover provides a totally specific and appealing length to your mini farm. By making use of vertical surfaces, you will be able to develop a diverse array of vegetation and make the most of even the smallest gardening regions.

CULTIVATING HERBS AND MEDICINAL PLANTS

Cultivating herbs and medicinal flowers in mini farming may be every worthwhile and sensible. Here's a guide to get you commenced out:

1. Choose Suitable Herbs and Medicinal Plants

Research: Learn about the herbs and medicinal flora which may be properly-right to your climate, soil kind, and to be had daytime.

Select Varieties: Choose types which might be compact and appropriate for area gardening or small areas.

2. Container Selection

Choose the Right Containers: Select containers with top drainage and ok space for the plant's root device. Use pots, raised beds, setting baskets, or vertical planters.

Well-Draining Soil: Use a properly-draining potting combo or soil mixture suitable for herbs. You also can combination compost to complement the soil.

three. Planting and Care

Planting Depth: Follow planting depth recommendations for every herb. Generally, plant seeds at a intensity it simply is two times the dimensions of the seed.

Watering: Keep the soil continuously wet but now not waterlogged. Herbs normally pick out out slightly drier situations as compared to three vegetables.

Sunlight: Most herbs thrive in whole solar, receiving at the least 6-eight hours of direct daytime every day.

Fertilization: Herbs normally do not require heavy feeding. Use a balanced natural fertilizer sparingly, as over-fertilization may additionally have an effect on flavor.

4. Pruning and Harvesting

Pruning: Regularly prune herbs to inspire bushy boom and prevent them from becoming leggy.

Harvesting: Harvest herbs through trimming the top increase, leaving part of the plant to hold growing. Harvest in the morning at the same time as the oils are maximum targeted.

Drying and Storing: Dry harvested herbs thru putting them in a fab, dark, properly-ventilated place. Store them in airtight bins in a dry, darkish place.

5. Common Herbs to Consider

Basil: Great for pesto and culinary makes use of.

Mint: Versatile for teas, drinks, and cakes.

Rosemary: Known for its aromatic leaves carried out in cooking.

Lavender: Used in aromatherapy and teas.

Chamomile: Known for its calming homes in teas.

Thyme: Used in savory dishes and as a medicinal herb.

6. Medicinal Plant Considerations

Research: Learn approximately the medicinal homes of the plants you're developing, and follow encouraged recommendations for utilization.

Quality: Focus on growing terrific flowers thru supplying proper care, due to the reality the efficiency of medicinal herbs often is predicated upon on their developing situations.

7. Organic Practices

Avoid Chemicals: Use natural practices to avoid chemical insecticides and fertilizers on your herbs and medicinal flora.

Cultivating herbs and medicinal flora for your mini farm can provide smooth and herbal additions in your food and fitness workout routines. With right care and interest, you may experience some of fragrant, flavorful, and useful plants proper at your fingertips.

Chapter 11: Raising Chickens and Small Livestock

Raising chickens and small livestock in mini farming can provide a sustainable deliver of eggs, meat, or even fertilizer on your garden. Here's a guide that will help you get began out out:

1. Check Local Regulations

Zoning Laws: Make outstanding your close by hints permit for raising chickens and small cattle on your region.

2. Choose the Right Livestock

Chickens: Start with a small form of hen breeds appropriate to your location and purpose. Research dual-cause breeds for every eggs and meat.

Small Livestock: Consider rabbits, quail, ducks, or guinea pigs as alternatives to chickens. Each has unique desires and benefits.

3. Housing and Shelter

Coop: Build or purchase a coop that gives secure haven, air flow, and protection from predators. Allow at least 2-three square feet of region steady with chook.

Nesting Boxes: Provide nesting boxes for chickens to put eggs.

4. Feeding and Watering

Quality Feed: Offer balanced feed suitable for the age and type of livestock you're raising.

Fresh Water: Provide smooth and smooth water commonly.

5. Health and Care

Regular Health Checks: Observe your cattle every day for symptoms and symptoms of contamination, harm, or pressure.

Veterinary Care: Establish a relationship with a veterinarian who is knowledgeable approximately livestock care.

Parasite Control: Implement everyday parasite manipulate measures as endorsed by the usage of a veterinarian.

6. Fencing and Security

Predator Prevention: Install proper fencing and solid enclosures to shield your farm animals from predators.

7. Waste Management

Composting: Livestock waste may be composted to create nutrient-wealthy compost for your lawn.

eight. Breeding and Reproduction

Breeding: If you would love to reproduce your livestock, research the specific goals and issues for a fulfillment breeding.

9. Ethical and Humane Practices

Animal Welfare: Provide a comfortable and humane surroundings to your livestock.

Ethical Treatment: Treat your livestock with respect and care inside the direction in their lives.

10. Learning and Research

Educate Yourself: Continuously teach yourself about the ideal wishes, behaviors, and care requirements of the farm animals you're elevating.

11. Local Resources

Local Farmers: Connect with nearby farmers or small-scale livestock keepers for advice and steering.

12. Start Small

Begin with Few: Start with a small variety of animals to have a look at the ropes and regularly amplify as you gain experience.

Raising chickens and small cattle can be a worthwhile trouble of mini farming, supplying you with a proper away connection for your meals sources and enhancing your sustainability efforts.

HARVESTING, PRESERVING, AND STORING YOUR PRODUCE

Mini farming is a fantastic manner to expand your very personal produce in a small vicinity. However, it is critical to comprehend the way to gain, keep, and store your produce to ensure that it lasts as long as viable. Here are some recommendations on a manner to do simply that:

1. Harvesting: The timing of your harvest is essential. You need to ensure you are deciding on your produce at the proper time. For example, tomatoes ought to be picked even as they're absolutely ripe, while lettuce ought to be picked before it

bolts. When harvesting your produce, use a sharp knife or scissors to reduce it off the plant. Be moderate so you do no longer harm the plant. It's moreover essential to gain your produce frequently to encourage greater increase.

2. Preserving: There are numerous methods to keep your produce, which consist of canning, freezing, and dehydrating. Canning is a top notch way to preserve vegetables like tomatoes and green beans. To can your produce, you can need a strain canner or a water bath canner. Follow the instructions carefully to make certain that your canned items are secure to devour. Freezing is a extraordinary possibility for stop end result like berries and peaches. To freeze your produce, wash and dry it thoroughly, then vicinity it in an airtight field or freezer bag. Dehydrating is a terrific alternative for herbs and end result like apples and

bananas. To dehydrate your produce, slice it thinly and location it in a dehydrator or in an oven set to a low temperature.

three. Storing: Once you've got preserved your produce, you want to save it nicely. Canned goods want to be stored in a cool, dry place. Make certain to label them with the date and contents so that you recognise when they have been canned. Frozen produce ought to be stored in a freezer at 0°F or under. Make certain to label them with the date and contents so that you understand what's in every bag or area. Dehydrated produce need to be stored in an hermetic container in a groovy, dry location. Make sure to label them with the date and contents so that you comprehend what's in every discipline.

four. Using: When you're organized to use your preserved produce, ensure you test the instructions for cooking or baking.

Canned items need to be heated to boiling earlier than ingesting. Frozen produce must be thawed earlier than using. Dehydrated produce may additionally furthermore need to be rehydrated in advance than the use of. To rehydrate your produce, soak it in water for some hours or in a single day.

By following those suggestions, you could make certain that your mini farm produces healthful and scrumptious end result and vegetables as a manner to remaining at some degree within the year. Remember to collect your produce regularly, keep it well, hold it in a cool, dry vicinity, and label it with the date and contents. With a hint little bit of strive, you may revel in your personal homegrown produce all three hundred and sixty five days spherical.

COMPOSITING FOR HEALTHY SOIL

Composting is an vital factor of mini farming that can help you create healthful soil for your flowers. Composting includes the machine of breaking down herbal be counted range, which incorporates meals scraps, outside waste, and awesome biodegradable materials, proper right right into a wealthy, nutrient-dense soil modification that may be used to beautify the quality of your soil.

To begin composting, you can want a compost bin or pile. You should purchase a compost bin or make one yourself using substances like wood pallets, twine mesh, or cinder blocks. Once you have were given your compost bin or pile set up, begin inclusive of natural rely to it. This can embody such things as fruit and vegetable scraps, coffee grounds, eggshells, grass clippings, leaves, and small twigs.

It's essential to maintain the proper balance of factors to your compost pile. Aim for a ratio of approximately 2 factors "brown" materials (which incorporates dried leaves or shredded newspaper) to at least one detail "green" materials (together with smooth grass clippings or vegetable scraps). Make positive to mix the materials in your compost pile often to promote even decomposition.

As your compost pile breaks down, it will generate warm temperature and in the long run alternate right into a darkish, crumbly cloth that appears and scents like soil. This completed compost can be introduced on your lawn beds or used as a top dressing round flowers. It's an superb supply of vitamins in your vegetation and may assist beautify soil shape, preserve moisture, and suppress weeds.

In addition to conventional composting, there are different strategies you could use to create healthful soil for your mini farm. For example, you may workout vermicomposting, which includes using worms to break down natural consider into compost. You also can make compost tea thru steeping finished compost in water anc the usage of the subsequent liquid as a fertilizer in your plant life.

Overall, composting is an smooth and powerful way to create healthful soil to your mini farm. By diverting natural waste from the landfill and turning it right proper right into a treasured useful aid, you could decorate the health and productivity of your lawn while reducing your environmental effect.

SUSTAINABLE PRACTICES AND RESOURCE MANAGEMENT

Sustainable practices and beneficial useful resource control are important factors of mini farming. Here are a few examples:

1. Conservation of water: Mini farmers can use diverse strategies to maintain water, together with using drip irrigation, mulching, and amassing rainwater. These practices can assist lessen water waste and make certain that plant life acquire the proper quantity of water.

2. Crop rotation: Mini farmers can rotate their vegetation to help save you soil depletion and decrease the risk of pests and illnesses. This exercising can also assist decorate soil fertility and boom yields.

3. Use of natural fertilizers: Mini farmers can use natural fertilizers, inclusive of compost and manure, to offer nutrients to their plant life. These fertilizers are sustainable and may assist enhance soil health over time.

4. Companion planting: Mini farmers can use associate planting to help control pests and improve soil fertility. Companion

planting consists of planting precise plant life collectively which have complementary dreams or benefits.

five. Integrated pest control: Mini farmers can use protected pest management (IPM) techniques to govern pests with out using volatile chemical substances. IPM involves using a aggregate of techniques, consisting of crop rotation, accomplice planting, and herbal predators, to control pests.

6. Energy conservation: Mini farmers can use electricity-green practices, which incorporates the use of sun-powered lighting and gadget, to reduce their power intake and environmental effect.

Overall, sustainable practices and useful useful useful resource manipulate are important for the prolonged-term fulfillment of mini farming. By the usage of these practices, mini farmers can create wholesome soil, hold resources, and decrease their environmental effect.

TROUBLESHOOTING COMMON CHALLENGES

1. Pests: Use organic pest manage techniques like neem oil, insecticidal cleansing cleansing cleaning soap, and associate planting to preserve pests at bay.

2. Lack of vicinity: Use vertical gardening strategies like trellising and hanging baskets to maximize your space. You also can use compact kinds of flora that absorb less location.

three. Lack of daylight: If you do now not have access to a sunny spot, undergo in thoughts the use of develop lighting to offer your plant life with correct sufficient mild.

4. Soil superb: Test your soil to see if it wishes any amendments like compost or fertilizer. You can also use raised beds or packing containers with tremendous soil to ensure your flowers have the nutrients they want.

5. Watering troubles: Make positive you are watering your flowers regularly and not over or underneath watering them. Consider the usage of a self-watering field or drip irrigation device to make watering less complicated and more inexperienced.

6. Climate demanding situations: Choose plants which might be well-appropriate in your weather and recall the use of season extenders like row covers or cold frames to boom your developing season.

By troubleshooting common disturbing conditions in mini farming, you may triumph over obstacles and experience a a fulfillment harvest.

SCALING UP AND EXPANDING YOUR MINI FARM

Scaling up and increasing your mini farm requires careful planning, investment in infrastructure, building relationships, and tracking improvement. Here are a few suggestions on a way to do it:

1. Start small: Before expanding your mini farm, ensure you've got the crucial competencies and property to govern a larger operation. Start with a small boom and frequently increase your manufacturing. This will assist you pick out out any challenges and expand answers earlier than making an investment in a bigger operation.

2. Plan in advance: Develop an prolonged-time period plan on your mini farm, which embody goals, timelines, and budgets. Consider factors like land availability, crop desire, and advertising techniques. This

plan need to guide your enlargement efforts and help you live targeted on your targets.

three. Invest in infrastructure: As you increase, you may want to put money into greater gear, system, and infrastructure like irrigation systems, garage centers, and fencing. These investments will help you boom your manufacturing functionality and decorate common overall performance.

4. Build relationships: Establish relationships with nearby farmers, markets, and clients to help you sell your products and construct a sustainable commercial business enterprise. Collaborating with one in every of a kind farmers will let you percent assets and know-how, on the identical time as building relationships with customers will can help you uncerstand their desires and alternatives.

five. Monitor your improvement: Keep track of your manufacturing, prices, and earnings to make certain that your mini farm is financially viable. Use this statistics to make informed picks about future increase. Regular tracking will assist you choose out regions for development and alter your method because of this.

Overall, scaling up and expanding your mini farm requires cautious making plans, funding in infrastructure, building relationships, and monitoring development. By following these guidelines, you may efficaciously extend your mini farm whilst preserving a focus on sustainability and profitability.

Chapter 12: Chickens

If you're interested in elevating chickens, there are various things you need to consider earlier than you get started out. Are you looking chickens for eggs, are you looking meat birds, or do you genuinely want a few for pets? Knowing what you need, will help you decide which chicks to buy.

If you are trying chickens for eggs, you have were given a few superb options. Different breeds of chickens lay one-of-a-type hues of eggs. I in my opinion ordered a selection for the a laugh of seeing all of the fantastically coloured chickens strolling round my outdoor and getting an array of egg shades and sizes. You can choose which breeds you need after which find out a hatchery to order them from, or a neighborhood breeder that you could really pressure over and choose them up. If you most effective want eggs, you do now not want any roosters for your bird house.

Some of the pleasant chickens for egg production and a pleasant form of egg shades are the Black Australop, Buff Orpingtons, Red Sex Link, White Leghorns and the Americaunas. There are many colours of Orpingtons that you may moreover have a take a look at. These are the breeds which you pay attention most human beings getting that need incredible medium to huge eggs in masses of colors, from slight brown to dark brown, lovely speckled, or blue and green eggs. Part of the a laugh of having chickens is discovering the types and getting the lovely egg colors.

There are execs and cons to ordering from a hatchery, shopping for network, or perhaps looking for from farm stores. You will see 3 options for every breed: roosters, hens, and right away run. The right now run are chicks that have not been sexed, so you are taking the risk of having a huge amount of roosters. Most neighborhood farms gained't intercourse the chicks, so that you each want to recognize what you're searching out otherwise you need to be inclined to risk getting roosters. A hatchery will supply chicks, which might be a bit extra high-priced, and a chunk greater demanding for the chicks, however you're confident hens excellent, (if that's what you order), or your cash decrease lower back.

If you are planning on proudly proudly owning meat birds, you need to buy them inside the spring, enhance them through the summer time after which cull them at the surrender of the only year. If it's miles strictly pets you want, make certain you buy a docile breed. Some chickens are each docile and top notch egg layers.

Before you purchased your chicks, you may want to make an indoor place to your babies to stay for as a minimum four weeks. You can use whatever from a huge plastic bath, a metal trough, or even a tall subject laid on a tarp. Heat will need to be supplied in the form of a warm temperature lamp or a brooder warm temperature plate. An oval trough works wonderful to area shavings within the backside, a heater on one stop and meals and water at the alternative. If the chicks are warmness, they'll in reality flow some distance from the warm temperature deliver. If they get cold, they will sincerely flow into closer to the warm temperature supply.

There are many alternatives to housing your chickens as quickly as they will be organized to be placed out of doors. You must make a hen coop out of many things. Part of the a laugh is analyzing what coop you need for the quantity of chickens you are searching out and the manner you want to build it. Or you may in reality buy one from a farm keep. Be powerful you've got were given sufficient nesting packing containers, a near water supply, and safety from predators even as you're finalizing coop plans.

It is essential to hold the feeders for chickens above the ground to avoid meals waste and to preserve mice and snakes out of the meals. Be certain to offer masses of clean water and if you add a dash of apple cider vinegar to the water it is stated to assist maintain your birds healthier.

Cattle

If you are making plans to elevate livestock, you will first want to prepare your pasture. Cows are strong, so a extremely good strong fence is vital. You can also need to take a soil test to appearance what minerals and hint elements are missing. Once that is completed, you could exercise the right fertilizer to get the effects you choice. Then seed consistent with your soil and climate. Managing your pasture is critical to its sturdiness.

The quality time to shop for farm animals is in the fall in advance than the farmer has to pay for feed at a few stage inside the winter months. You gets a better deal on cows and calves that have been raised on pasture than in case you wait to shop for until spring. Beef cattle will do well in most climates. If you are confined in vicinity, an extremely good rule of thumb is one cow steady with acre. Cattle do well in most any climate so long as they have got secure haven.

Shelter is essential for max cattle. Some animals want greater safe haven than others. Horses and cows need a barn, however donkeys simplest need a 3 sided safe haven to get below within the course of lousy weather. No rely the animal, make certain you have got got a close to deliver of water and the potential to get food in your animals at a few level inside the wintry climate. A combination of grains together with barley and wheat paintings well at the same time as added for your cow's food. Cattle want day by day get admission to to between 1 and a couple of gallons of smooth water constant with a hundred kilos of body weight. If your cows have pasture land, they might live to tell the tale with the resource of and large from consuming grass. Use a hay rack or clean food box to provide your livestock grain. If the grain gets wet or moldy it can make your farm animals very unwell. Feeding your farm animals grain will help them come to be acquainted with you and assist you form a bond. Whistle or name for them to come lower returned as you are commencing the grain and very quickly they will start to respond to the sound of your voice. Cows furthermore need salt of their diet. You can positioned a salt combination near their food, or simply located out a salt and mineral block for them to lick.

Cattle vaccinations can help protect them from illnesses which incorporates blackleg or BVD. Some vets will promote the vaccinations for you to deliver yourself and a few will come out on your farm and vaccinate your herd. Whatever you choose out, it's miles a high-quality concept to vaccinate. If you should take advantage of your cows, ask your vet about timing amongst vaccinating and milking.

Cattle are herd animals and do not do properly on my own. If you want cows to your mini farm, make certain to get at the least , They get lonely if they are by myself. If you have got calves, deliver in a few mature cows to keep them calm.

Having a few cows to your mini farm is a exquisite choice in case you want clean milk or if you plan on elevating your personal beef.

Chapter 13: Goats

Raising goats on small farms is a developing enterprise organization. Goats are raised for masses motives which embody milk, meat, or certainly as pets. Raising goats is a lot of a laugh; however it does require records of what you need to raise satisfied, healthful goats.

Just like livestock, goats are herd animals and ought to have a pal to thrive. Goats can be with exclusive livestock, but however need a few different goats with them. If you have a predator hassle, setting a donkey in together together with your goats will hold the predators away. The donkey will defend the goats as long as they may be the pleasant donkey in the field.

It isn't advocated to place multiple breeding donkeys in with the goats because the male donkey will defend the girl donkey and no longer fear as a bargain approximately the goats. In reality, in case your goats have infants, the male donkey might also moreover furthermore see the babies as predators and kill them to protect the girl donkey. So when you have breeding goats, do now not positioned more than one donkey in with them for protection.

Goats don't require plenty to get started out. The four maximum vital topics that you'll be wanting for goats are secure haven, fencing, meals, and primary healthcare. Goats do now not need to get wet, so it is crucial to have a dry place for them to get in during inclement climate. They can use the equal form for colour. Goats want a huge area for shelter It is critical to their time-venerated health,

Fencing is of the maximum significance almost about raising goats. Your fence line should be robust or your goats might be out and down the road in a flash. Goats need to climb to get to leaves up excessive. It looks like they could as a substitute consume the higher leaves, than consume those which might be on their degree. Cattle panels art work nicely or a strong goat fence.

Goats will forage for food if it's far available, however you may maximum actually need an incredible mineral block and brought hay at the same time as important. If you have got were given wood for your goat pen, positioned a protector throughout the trunk or the goat will consume the whole lot, which includes the trunk of the tree.

If you have were given a small vicinity and also you want goats, an splendid manner to transport will be the miniature, pygmy, or bypass breed. Pygmy/Nigerian Dwarf crosses are excellent little goats for amusing and for pets. With the crosses, you get a robust little goat from the pygmy genes and the lovable sun shades and blue eyes from the Nigerian Dwarf breed. If you bottle feed a infant goat, it becomes like a doggy and look at you around anywhere you move. These small goats are wonderful amusing to examine, particularly if you have timber toys for them to climb on.

With the pygmy and ND mixes, you come to be with a lovely sort of colorations of fur and eyes. If you are making plans on breeding your goats and promoting them, a tri-colored, blue eyed goat will convey in extra money than a single colored, brown eyed goat. So if your plan is to breed for income, ensure your greenback or does have the coloring you want and having blue eyes is a large bonus. If making a decision you want a small herd of goats, keep in mind which you most effective want one male to 50 ladies. As the does infant, or have infants, you could want to promote your bucklings or wether them if you plan on maintaining them. It is quite smooth to band a buckling, which turns him right right into a wether. This will save you you from having a couple of breeding greenback in your herd. You should buy the materials to band your individual men at most farm supply stores. You don't need to band them till they're at least ten weeks antique or it could cause urinary troubles.

If you are elevating goats for pets, every special element you could want to recall is whether or not or not you need polled goats, because of this no horns, or horned goats. It is simply only a rely of choice. Goats don't typically use their horns for something however safety from predators. Some human beings pick to buy infants an amazing way to both be obviously polled, meaning they'll now not expand horns, or babies which have been disbudded.

Disbudding a goat is a simple technique that your vet or a skilled farmer can do. You can also ask your vet if there is someone they advise in your location that does disbudding. I first-rate disbud if someone requests it and they may be seeking out the little one goat as a bottle little one. Disbudding is the technique of cauterizing the small horn buds while the infant goat is just a few days antique. It is done in a rely of seconds and doesn't appear to purpose any residual ache to the goat. Some humans undergo in thoughts it cruel, however it isn't clearly any excellent than docking a dog's tail. It is truly a undergo in thoughts of choice. If you are shopping for bottle toddlers and elevating them as pets and you have have been given small children or grandchildren you can pick them not to have horns.

If you're breeding your goats, you need to offer the babies a CDT shot at 30 days antique and some other at 60 days vintage. After that, you can need to offer them a CDT vaccination as quickly as a 12 months. You can purchase the CDT and syringes at any feed save, or pay your vet to offer them. All adult goats will want a each year CDT shot, additionally. This prevents them from getting unwell and doubtlessly passing the infection directly to their infants. You can even need to deworm your goats. Some people prefer to laptop virus each yr and a few favor to deworm satisfactory while essential. You can take a fecal sample to your vet and they will take a look at it and let you recognize if there are worms and if so, what type they'll be. If in reality considered one of your goats has worms, opportunities are your whole herd will. You will need to deworm the whole herd. It isn't a tough method, it is a depend of squirting the dewormer from a syringe into your goats mouth. There are matters which might be available to have spherical in case considered one in every of your animals receives sick. Always have rubber gloves reachable. Then counting on the animal, ask your vet what styles of primary remedies you should maintain accessible. Those topics may be a lifestyles saver in a time of need. The list will range from animal to animal.

Gardening

A lot of human beings develop their very own greens. If they live in the city they may have area vegetation or increase a outdoor garden . People who stay in the america of the us can also have huge vegetable gardens. One difficulty most human beings have in commonplace is that they opt for sparkling produce over store offered produce. If you've got by no means tasted garden clean meals, you will be amazed through the flavors.

While mini farm gardens may be any duration, they tend to be large out in the usa of america due to the fact greater people need to live off the land as an lousy lot as possible. If you have in no manner had a lawn earlier than, it is endorsed to begin small on the same time as you test gardening and amplify as you experience snug. Location is essential to having a garden that produces the high-quality great veggies. There are a few subjects to preserve in mind on the identical time as selecting your garden region. It wants to be in a sunny spot that drains nicely. If you live in a place with very moist soil that doesn't drain nicely, you want to recall constructing a raised bed garden. You need an area with the most nutrient rich soil and preferably now not very windy.

If you choose a small garden, it's miles crucial to choose the right flowers. Start with vegetation that you truly enjoy ingesting or the ones which is probably costly to buy. Use accomplice planting techniques thru placing small, rapid-growing plants amongst huge, slower developing ones. In doing this, you can have much less wasted place. Growing on a small scale within the beginning makes it less complicated to preserve the garden region weed free. Another benefit of accomplice planting is that you may plant

plant life on your lawn so that you can enchantment to beneficial insects who will honestly shield your flora or draw pests a protracted manner from your garden and for your vegetation.

As you're making plans your lawn there are various alternatives to remember. Each has its personal advantages. If you're beginning small, you could want to test planting a raised bed garden. You receiver's need to prepare the ground for planting, you definitely build the raised mattress additives and upload your soil, mulch anc something else you pick out to install your soil earlier than you plant. If you have a larger lawn in thoughts, you may want to go along with the traditional row garden. You will but need to mix the soil with mulch and distinctive minerals to put together it for planting, but you received't must construct the above floor beds. Either desire will paintings in your small garden place.

If you're an inexperienced gardener, you likely need first of all flora that you can seed proper into the floor. Here is a list of the top 10 simplest vegetables to growth yourself.

1. Lettuce - Lettuce may be grown three hundred and sixty five days round in climates that aren't too hot. There are many types of lettuce from shades of green and pink to leaves of all one-of-a-kind shapes. Lettuce is a plant that can be lessen because it grows, so you can experience numerous plants out of 1 lettuce plant.

2. Green Beans - Green beans will develop in pretty hundreds any soil. The beans will repair the nitrogen as they grow. If you're planting in a confined region, a pole range will prevent area

because it grows on a trellis. All beans are fast growers and do higher in a heat, wet soil.

3. Peas - Peas can be planted as soon as you could work the soil. They may be planted in early spring, even in advance than the very last frost. To have a non-stop harvest of peas, plant a row or of peas and then weeks later plant every different row or . You can hold to try this through spring, but no later than mid June.

four. Radishes - Like peas, radishes can be planted as fast as you could paintings the soil. They also are fast growing and can be harvested in 24 days. You can plant your radishes together together with your carrots and the quick growing radishes will assist split the soil for the slow growing carrots. When you harvest your radishes, the carrots will fill in the row.

five. Carrots - This is another vegetable that may be planted early, as they're in a position to take care of a frost. Carrots are clean to grow if you have the proper sort of soil. They want a sandy soil in case you need to with out hassle increase, due to the fact they aren't strong and will become deformed inside the occasion that they change into a rock or different hard surfaces in the floor. So till your carrot place nicely and upload some sand to help make the soil less tough to control. As your carrots begin poking through the ground, make certain to thin them very well. They want their very own vicinity to expand and unfold.

Chapter 14: Fruit Trees

Having an orchard on your small farm isn't always out of reap. Normally whilst people consider an orchard, they recollect many acres of tall fruit trees

which you need to climb a ladder to benefit. That is not the case in any respect. With the proper method and care, you may increase fruit wooden which can be no taller than a person and grow the same fruit as a everyday period fruit tree may also want to.

When planning your orchard, you need to begin with what fruit you would like to enlarge and the best shape of that fruit. You can choose any fruit, provided it suits your place and developing conditions. The high-quality difference in a massive fruit orchard and your small farm orchard is that you're going to teach your timber to a small stature by using way of pruning. All you want to recognise is that if the rootstock of the tree is suitable on your growing conditions.

It is taught which you need to plant wood in the fall and prune in the spring. For your fruit timber, you want to reserve a more youthful, naked root tree in past due spring. The extra youthful naked root tree will do higher with the excessive pruning than a properly set up fruit tree may.

Selecting a site for your timber isn't always all people-of-a-type than choosing a domain to your garden. You want them in which they may get masses of solar, at the least six hours a day. Make positive water is consequences available in your bushes and that they're in a available location. You don't need to be taking walks a long manner sporting on your fruit harvest. Unlike regular fruit orchards, your wood do no longer want to be planted a ways apart. Since you'll be pruning them right proper right down to period, you can plant your wooden as near as three ft aside.

In order to preserve your timber smaller, the number one pruning will appear to be very painful. You will prune the trunk all of the manner down to approximately toes immoderate. This will restriction the vertical developing capacity of the tree and preserve the branches developing out in location of the trunk developing up. This reduce desires to be made right after the tree is planted. Then you can prune out undesirable branches at some degree inside the summer season, so that you can teach the tree to restrict its increase.

After you have got finished the initial pruning through the summer, the rest is easy. Other than a hint mulch round the lowest, and watering, in case you stay in a very dry weather, you shouldn't need to do something else. With this technique, you may see an fit for human intake crop of fruit as early as the 0.33 12 months. With a hint pruning each summer season, you may preserve your bushes healthful and the exceptional duration for your small farm.

www.ingramcontent.com/pod-product-compliance
Lightning Source LLC
Chambersburg PA
CBHW071444080526
44587CB00014B/1983